Game Addiction

The Experience and the Effects

NEILS CLARK *and*
P. SHAVAUN SCOTT

McFarland & Company, Inc., Publishers
Jefferson, North Carolina, and London

LIBRARY OF CONGRESS CATALOGUING-IN-PUBLICATION DATA

Clark, Neils.
    Game addiction : the experience and the effects / Neils Clark
and P. Shavaun Scott.
        p.   cm.
    Includes bibliographical references and index.

    ISBN 978-0-7864-4364-2
    softcover : 50# alkaline paper ∞

    1. Video game addiction.   2. Video games — Psychological
aspects.   3. Video games and children.   4. Video games and
teenagers.   I. Scott, P. Shavaun.   II. Title.
RC569.5.V53C53   2009
616.85'84 — dc22   2009012386

British Library cataloguing data are available

Cover illustration ©2009 Brand X Pictures

Manufactured in the United States of America

*McFarland & Company, Inc., Publishers
    Box 611, Jefferson, North Carolina 28640
    www.mcfarlandpub.com*

NEILS:

To Alysa Majer

SHAVAUN:

To Mike,
for ensuring I am never without the means
to enact every random creative thought,
and for forcing me to do the things
I swear I have no time to do.

And to Matt & Dan,
for teaching me how to be a highly competent elf.

TABLE OF CONTENTS

That which is dreamed
Can never be lost,
can never be
un-dreamed.
...
Only the phoenix arises
and does not descend.
And everything changes.
And nothing is truly lost.
— Neil Gaiman

For the probability of error increases with the scope of the undertaking, and any man who sells his soul to synthesis will be a tragic target for a myriad merry darts of specialist critique. "Consider," said Ptah-Hotep five thousand years ago, "how thou mayest be opposed by an expert in council. It is foolish to speak on every kind of work." — Will Durant

PREFACE
by Neils Clark

I stared transfixed. A six-hundred-dollar computer monitor sat on a dingy hardwood floor, and I knew that I had been hunched over it for the better part of that day, most of the week, and all that summer. I was playing one video game twenty hours a day, and it seemed normal up until that night. There was probably an hour of silent staring. I left for graduate school the next week, without a computer and unable to shake that night's feeling of shock.

My name is Neils, and even though I'll tell you a little bit about the people I've murdered, the woman I married, and the millions that I've made in video games, this book isn't strictly about any one person's story. This book was born out of an attempt to make sense of gaming addictions through research. As it matured, it became clear that tens, if not hundreds, of millions of people around the world were killing, working, marrying, and feeding on video games. Their stories, in many cases told through their eyes, are used to augment and clarify the game-effects research accumulating across fields that rarely attempt communication, let alone collaboration.

Right now there's really no way to know whether video games, television, or even the world's massive entertainment culture will be a force for positive or negative change. What we do know is that things are changing. An eleven-year-old Vietnamese boy strangled an 81-year-old woman for the equivalent of five U.S. dollars, then buried her under a thin layer of sand in front of his house. Questioned by police, he said that he needed the money for items in a video game. This coin has two sides. An eight-year-old Norwegian boy saved his younger sister's life by putting his own life at risk, threatening an attacking moose and then feigning death once it began attacking him. Questioned later, he said that he learned those skills in a video game.

For me, starting to play too much didn't have much to do with the usual explanations; my excesses weren't attributable to some manic imbalance, nor a childhood that was too psychologically traumatic to mention. My childhood was charmed. Though I can't say for certain where problems with gaming started, I do remember one summer when I was about nine. My friend down the street, Jason, had a brand new Super Nintendo. I remember greeting him at the door, sitting down to play for a few hours and then refusing to get up when everyone left to play with water guns. Something about Mario seduced me — God only knows what. The thing that I do remember is Jason's father coming home. I remember the hot sting of embarrassment when he asked why I wasn't playing with his son. I don't remember my reply — but I do remember what he did: Nothing.

This book is neither pro-games nor anti-games. Above all it's about how we *experience* games and what they really mean to us. What's happening can't be solved by just loving or hating the technologies surrounding the worlds online. We have to understand them and, as much as possible, enter this next generation with more personal responsibility in using them and more professional understanding in making them. What's drawn a few types of people of my generation into games — is already pulling almost the entirety of the coming generation into the offspring of games. We can't take back any of these technologies and addiction is just one blip on the radar of how they will change our world. But for better or for worse?

I don't think that gamers are bad, because I don't think that I am bad. Gamers have experiences the likes of which very few people in our history have been afforded, wherein they can play the parts of good, evil, or morally grey characters. The theatre is digital, but the other puppeteers still bleed when their hearts and minds are cut too deeply. Gamers have had incredible experiences; they could do incredible things.

In his book on "the virtual worlds exodus," Ted Castronova was surprised that the crew of the starship *Enterprise*, in the famous television show *Star Trek: Next Generation*, only used the holodeck every so often. If you're not familiar with the holodeck, it was the ultimate video game: It was photorealistic, all of the senses were stimulated, and it could recreate any scenario imaginable. In a simple room, real-feeling and convincing events could be re-created. With the ability to enter their favorite experiences as much as they wanted, whenever they wanted, Castronova uses economic theories to say that there's no reason for the crew to have been anywhere *but* the holodeck. Since we already have this technology in today's games, he says, real life will have to compensate by becoming more satisfying — otherwise nobody is going to spend time running the real-life starship. People won't engage in society as we know it, because it "won't be for them."

Wrong. I've played with the people who can't leave today's Holodeck, and it's rarely a happy scene. I've seen a friend — a doctor — give up one of the world's most prestigious residencies only to move into one of California's most run-down suburbs. I've smelled people who left their dormitory rooms to buy Husky burgers, but not to attend their final exams or to relieve themselves. Some of my best friends in real life started out as my favorite rivals in video games. I've met some gamers who will leave profoundly positive marks on this world, but I've seen many more who are consumed by the game and then matriculated into the establishment. They don't demand that life become more exciting, that it better suit their needs. They lose themselves, accepting the rank and file when they were just months from saving lives as doctors and establishing themselves as professionals. And that's without a holodeck. That's today.

The crew of the starship *Enterprise* uses the holodeck responsibly because they understand how it works. They know the risks, and they know how to balance reality with entertainment. That knowledge is not free. It is a hard-won understanding that most regular video game players don't have yet — just like we don't have phasers, warp speed or anything else from the *Star Trek* universe. We're just not there. Most people today don't understand that video games are here to inspire us to make a better reality. They use today's entertainment to replace reality, rather than to feel its cool uncertainty or face its subtle antagonists. Great entertainment can keep us collected and happy in a world where every day is more complex than the day before, but without understanding it beforehand we risk losing ourselves. This isn't so much the case with traditional media like books or television. This is a risk inherent to video games, one that's only going to grow alongside more sophisticated entertainment. We should definitely take hints from virtual worlds, if those systems show us how to make life better. What we can't do is give up on the world that we already have.

At least 126 million people in the U.S. are playing video games, and the American Medical Association has reported estimates that 10 to 15 percent of Americans are addicted. That's 12.6 to 18.9 *million* people in the U.S. alone, and these numbers *pale* in comparison to the millions of parents, spouses, game developers, educators, and therapists who share many of the consequences.

They also pale compared to other countries. The Korean federal government recently released a statement estimating that at least 2.2 million young gamers are addicted and that the affliction is pandemic. The Chinese government expects far more, old and young, as they have over 140 million broadband connections. The Singaporean parliament was in a state of panic in late 2007. This isn't something that the world can solve by burying its collective head in the sand.

One of the most venerated media theorists of all time, Marshall McLuhan, once said, "There can only be disaster arising from unawareness of the causalities and effects inherent in our technologies." Obviously, it's high time we understand his causalities and effects. Whether we like it or not, games have become a part of our world. At some point in the near future, most everyday people aren't going to "play" because it's fun, or because they want to. It won't even be addiction. These games are about to hit the mainstream, becoming a serious meeting-place for regular people around the world. In certain countries, and in certain generations, they already are.

This book has attempted, as much as possible, to take a multidisciplinary approach. Where Shavaun's research as a psychotherapist has brought her to study varied approaches to the treatment of gaming pathologies in children and adults, I have similarly taken a broad approach to understanding the many rich draws to worlds online. Together we've worked to reconcile the divide between clinicians and academics, using accepted and respected research in neuroscience, media studies, developmental psychology, anthropology, behavioral psychology, communication, interpersonal neurobiology, literary theory, and many of the other fields where the groundwork for understanding games is being laid. The aim of this book is to serve as an intermediary between academics from these varied disciplines and professional venues; the tone has been kept as practical and straightforward as possible. Case studies, anecdote, and personal example are applied in order to further clarify relationships between issues traditionally deemed too prohibitively complex for out-discipline research.

The first three chapters provide the basic background on the nature of gaming, how gamers play, and why gamers play. This background is absolutely necessary to more fully grasp how and why addiction can grab certain players. Chapter One, "The Digital Living Room," explores the fundamental growth of games and addiction, explaining why their underlying technologies will soon be available to most regular media consumers. Chapter Two, "Media Experience and Real Illusion," examines the history of various media, with special attention to how things like literature and film physically massage the senses. Chapter Three, "Why They Play," looks at various ways of explaining basic player motivations.

The last three chapters expand on knowledge of why gaming experiences are complex, showing how addiction can develop. Chapter Four, "Anatomy of a Game Addiction," takes major elements utilized in the contemporary treatment and understanding of addictions, using them to shed more light on excesses observed among gamers. Chapter Five, "Games Are Not Babysitters," explains how children are unique in the ways they integrate the gaming experience. Chapter Six, "The Road Ahead," steps back, connecting some of the book's main concepts in order to lightly survey other possible effects of game technologies.

This book, like many, was only possible through the help of many, many people. I would like to acknowledge Alysa Majer, Dennis Clark, and Marjie Clark. Also Dr. Thomas Malaby and Dr. Jerald Block, M.D., for suggestions that revealed pathways I'd been on and where those could lead. Mark Hukill, for having the rarely found courage to be sharply honest. Dr. Aaron Delwiche and Jennifer Lloyd, without whom an adventure in studying games would never have begun.

For graciously giving of their time, stories and insight: Dr. Angeline Khoo, Dave Yeager, Andrew Bradbury, Kateri Snyder, Ji Hoon Oh, Jeff McNeill, Florence Chee, Linn Sovig, Nikki Inderlied, Max Meyer, Shawnda Blansjaar, Richard Pendlebury, Jared Norberg, Cameron Bunch, Morgan

Romine, Sunni Giordano, Kate Hartley, Philip Magistrado, Robert Anthony Lopez, and Amanda Barrera.

Also, our sincere thanks to all of the gamers and parents whose stories and case studies appear anonymously.

Last but certainly not least, I would like to acknowledge the pair whose documentary planted the inspiration for this project, Shavaun Scott and Michael Balzer.

Names and identifying details from Shavaun's clinical cases have been changed to protect the anonymity of individuals. All other interviews depict the names and nationalities of real gamers.

One

THE DIGITAL LIVING ROOM

Whether your best friends live in Sydney, Mumbai or just a few miles away, get ready for a cheap face-to-face conversation, from the comfort of your own living room. With a few clicks of the remote, you and your global friends might opt for chit-chat, conversation over a game of cards, a good movie, or your favorite shows. However far-fetched that might seem, it's happening in video games right now. Instead of normal leisure, gamers and their good friends are slaying dragons and battling aliens. Hundreds of thousands of people are playing inside the digital living room right this second. On a whim they can play and connect with friends from around the world, in ways that seem like science fiction to many.

You're not going insane; this is still a book about game addiction. This book is not a sensational rant about how deranged players are suckling on convenient heroin dispensers. Nor is it the opposite, a selectively blind eye to what games are and how they encourage sometimes obscene levels of play. Current research says a few things about what drives people into their illusionary environs, be they books, games or anything else. This so-called digital living room is where our story begins.

If you cracked open this book because someone you know could be playing too much, then the first thing to know is that you are not alone. Game addiction, spurred by any of the causes discussed herein, likely affects a few million internationally — very probably more.

The second thing to know is that gaming technology is about to be part of *everybody's* entertainment, everybody's lives. Game makers are working hard to make games simple, straightforward, and *meaningful* for everyone. These new gadgets won't just be for people with the arcane knowledge of technological mysticism; they'll be for everyone.

The third and final thing you should know is that these new entertainment technologies aren't automatically addictive. Addiction is a nice, simple word, but the hooks drawing people into contemporary media are complex. Human beings get tripped up because video games provide draws that most people don't yet know how to balance. Society has barely been exposed to them, let alone their propensity for pulling the rug out from under a person. This precarious situation isn't a cause to be angry or frightened. It's just a call to quickly understand a beast that is quickly manifesting itself.

Over two decades ago, Michael Crichton wrote, "There are plenty of places left in the world where one can live a nineteenth-century life, an eighteenth-century life, or even a tenth-century life — but few people rush to live in them."[1] Things like games and computers aren't evil by nature. They're a new part of our world: the state of the art for art. Games are "addicting" people without recognizable susceptibilities because this fixation on taking in media plays to many new susceptibilities.

There are a lot of tangible reasons to read books, listen to radio, watch television and so on. Some reasons are more subtle; many are just outside of one's usual perception. Some have everything to do with human perception. Imagine that your favorite story could go on forever. Then, imagine that you are the main character. Now imagine that you can choose between thousands of these stories; in essence that you can pick a never-ending story that's right for you. This is what sophisticated games are: a place where we, you and me, control the story and plot for ourselves. What we've got in video games can *absolutely* be a problem, but addiction doesn't appear out of thin air. Balancing these different realities is an altogether new skill, one that too many of today's gamers have learned the hard way. Some might never learn.

When today's players lose their sense of balance and perspective, there's almost never one single culprit. Rather, they experience a perfect storm; the game and the gamer each come to the table with a mass of factors that can help or hinder healthy playing. In the gamer, physiological addiction can originate from the chemical and psychological reactions to playing specific games. These vary dramatically between different players. Serious mental or physical problems can also make an imbalance more likely. The gamer aside, there are as many legitimate reasons to play games as there are people, and the gaming experience looks at how games go about stoking the fires in different gamers. Physical and cognitive immersion can naturally keep players "within" games longer than they had anticipated. For specific people, certain games can be more powerful than others; designers work hard to make them compelling, satisfying, fun even. They're so much fun, at times, that gamers can play to the point where they're making real problems for themselves. These problems, ironically, often spur players to want games all the more.

This is why understanding game addiction is important for everybody: as legitimate as it may be for an individual to embargo games for themselves, media has an effect on everybody. The presence or absence of any one person in any one reality changes things. There are wholly new elements to society being introduced by advanced games. A great many of these can be better understood through exploring the excesses being called game addiction. Understanding how gaming alters the senses, what drives it and its broad effects on life, online or off, isn't just for the academics or the mental health professionals. It's useful for any person consuming any type of media.

A Perfect Storm

"For me, playing computer games is almost meditative ... I don't think of bills, work or stressful things," says Max. "I might not answer my phone in time, but I do respond to my child crying."

Meet Norwegian gamer Max Meyer. At 28 he balances work, school, his wife, his newborn child, and video games. Like most gamers in today's digital living room, Max takes his commitments to other players seriously. He doesn't let gaming come before real life, but he loves every second that he gets to spend playing with his friends online. For some gamers, that sense of balance is a hard-won skill.

"I ended up playing about 10 hours a day on average," he says, remembering the back-and-forth needed to stay competitive in MMORPGs. "Suffice it to say, this took a heavy toll on my university performance that semester."

This is a pattern that all too many gamers can relate to. Games give us more reasons than ever to love entertainment, and so finding the right balance is a challenge. Max is lucky; while he will probably always love games, his sense of responsibility (and his wife) will help him to keep all of these worlds in perspective. "The important change for me is that I have quit playing all day, every day," he says, though he worries about the next time he'll feel the pressure to keep up. "Still, I have my wife to catch me if things get out of hand."

Some gamers are neither that lucky nor that mature; they can lose their grip when these two realities start to compete with one another. Ultimately it takes two to tango — this addiction takes a gamer and a game. Every person is different, and we've all got unique strengths and susceptibilities. When unique people play unique games, the result is always a unique experience. No one factor is going to instantaneously create an addict. Rather, the game experience hits everyone as a perfect storm; many small things combine, creating a force that can be unstoppable. The storm's high seas and gusts are the many draws to gaming. The ship is the person playing, along with his or her many unique susceptibilities. Gamers who sail flimsy boats into treacherous waters will too often sink. At the same time, even "unsinkable" ships go under when they underestimate the sea, venturing without charts, without knowledge of the tides and without advance warning on foul weather. Many players don't have the effective restraint or support structure of players like Max Meyer. Without understanding themselves and their entertainment, they risk losing themselves in the perfect storm.

From relatively new ways to understand brain scanning and brain chemistry, to the decades of research in fields like psychology and media, we can track a number of characteristics that make games as alluring as they are. We can also identify what they are not. Video games aren't a silver bullet, one whose harsh waters rope in any soul. Games combine many different technologies which we have already researched. For example, we know that human eyes are particularly bad at telling the difference between real images and images presented on a television set.[2] When the show is over, our brains can tell us that the anchors for the evening news weren't speaking to us directly. However, our brains aren't always tuned into that *during* the experience.[3]

Our brains can get caught up in the moment. If nothing interrupts an exciting image, then we may not be able to put the image in context until after the excitement has passed.[4] When we're caught up in watching a car chase on our favorite show, our adrenaline might pump as though we were watching a real speeding car. If our favorite character crashes that car and dies, then we might feel the drama as though a real person had died—at least, so long as the television is turned on.

But television doesn't usually addict us; at best a television watcher might get grumpy if they get caught in traffic and miss a show. So why is traffic torture for some gamers? There's more than one story out there of hasty gamers who lose control of their vehicles and flip them over or collide.[5] One of my favorites involves two hours of sleep, a brand-spanking-new BMW and no loss of life. When the events inside a game have you running on little or no sleep, rushing home for more and putting other people at risk, then something is wrong. But it's a level of responsibility that we could be seeing more and more. When a player gets to this point they've graduated beyond the level of liking a game for its colorful characters and stunning chase scenes.

One part of gaming addiction does have to do with a new and improved living room, but the other part has to do with neuroscience and psychology. Game addiction is a process where the gamer and the game work together, changing the brain over a long process of small steps.[6] Some oversimplified examples might involve a gamer who's had a particularly bad day, or somebody whose particular brain can get a lot of excitement from gaming. In both cases they're more likely to play. In neither case will gaming be good or bad in and of itself.[7] Certain pieces of physiology can have a persuasive influence in how people play, and certain skills help them to stay balanced and emotionally healthy.[8] Games can even help us to stay emotionally healthy, but gamers need to understand how to balance their play.[9] With those skills, gamers are far less likely to gorge themselves and start a cycle of constantly increasing play.

With a gaming experience that appears to offer so much to satisfy physical and mental needs, that cycle can all-too-frequently spiral out of control.[10] Gamers with predispositions and susceptibilities have a hard time controlling their play, and too much gaming, no matter how rewarding it feels at the time, can open the door for more and bigger problems. Ultimately, our way of telling that someone has a problem isn't that they magically qualify for the label "addict"; it's when they're having serious real-world problems. A major part of staying healthy is the ability to live a functional, balanced life and to maintain a healthy mind, strong physical body, and positive relationships.

This is the primary way in which mental health professionals identify and define "addiction": when a single behavior starts to transform business-as-usual into out-of-service. If somebody isn't eating, isn't going to work, and they've been so hooked to the computer that they've let the cat die, then these might just be signs that the game is interfering with their lives. If the cat really is dead, then it's safe to say that this process of addiction is well on its way.

Game addiction is usually no one thing, but rather a spellbinding firestorm; a satisfying game bombards a gamer's psyche with those elements it's always seeking, as well as those it never knew existed. The human eye can have a hard time looking away from some things. The more that a player disregards reality, the greater the storm's power to enthrall.

This whole process has humble roots in older forms of entertainment, despite the fact that they tend not to inspire such spectacular devotion. While there are insatiable bookworms and 40-year-old sci-fi junkies in mom and dad's basement, things like books and television rarely make it impossible for someone to hold down a job, or to leave the house for more than a couple of hours. Games spice up media in complex ways, but the new flavors can be introduced in two major enticements.

The Secret Ingredients

I want to share with you one of my proudest moments ever. Not just a moment in games, but one of my proudest moments *ever*. There was such an intense sense of elation that all I wanted to do was to scream in triumph. Despite the amazing sights on the computer monitor, I couldn't exactly join my fellows in beating my chest with a cry. My parents were sleeping.

The shrieks of other players rang through my headphones, and I'm positive that the heart of every person there was beating out of control. We all watched with morbid fascination as the body of C'thun, the evil god, fell to the floor of his ancient temple. His vicious tentacles slumped, his massive eye long destroyed, black smoke spilling from his belly and into the center of the room. Moments later we watched with equal fascination as the three pieces of treasure he guarded were given to the most dedicated of us. There were forty heroes in all, and we had spent the last two months on just this *one* fight. Through a mixture of teamwork, skill, and preparation, we had succeeded. There was a palpable sense of brotherhood. A sense of completion that none of us could probably ever fully explain.

Few others in the game World of Warcraft ever defeated C'thun. Fighting him requires devoted discipline and teamwork, and most of his attacks kill a character no matter how many hours or days a gamer has spent making themselves more powerful. Besides, why would today's players ever invest that kind of effort in defeating C'thun, what with all of the fresher battles and better treasures in the Arena, the reintroduced Naxxramas, Ulduar or any other level 80 raid?

It's a shame, really. Of all the times I've stood with gamers and defeated an enemy, the fight against C'thun is always what surfaces in my mind as the most indescribable. However much it "only happened in a game," that night stands out as a milestone accomplishment in my real life. The fight didn't happen in reality, per se, but neither was it something that just happened in a game. Ask the real people who were there.

We players aren't just connecting to these other people. On a whim, we step inside places and situations which just aren't easy to re-create in nature. Some of them aren't even possible. When we say that games are going to radically change what happens inside the living room, or even in everyday social spaces, it's not just that some of these games put us on a virtual couch with Bob from Ireland. "Game" is one word that refers to many technologies.

It's understandable that a lot of people would find it easier to think that all games are the same, and natural for humans to use a blanket term like "game." That misconception is a major stumbling block. If you imagine for a second two avid gamers, you might see each sitting at a separate computer, and in each case the game has completely sucked them in. Staring over their shoulders, you might not be able to tell the difference. Even though most people wouldn't be able to either, these two could be playing for *completely* different reasons. If getting hooked on a game were a simple matter of one or two mischievous puzzle pieces, then we wouldn't need a book to tell us about game addiction. You'd just have to take those problem pieces out.

There are a lot of things that take games beyond other forms of entertainment, but we should start with the two most basic. First, games aren't as passive as other media. Second, they connect us to other living people.[11] Games are more advanced than even most gamers would probably realize. Gaming technologies have been perfected for years, giving gamers the ability to interact and socialize on an extremely advanced level. Technologies for interaction and connection worked to set the foundations for the gaming experience that we've got today. These two secret ingredients will get us started on why this word "game" no longer really does justice to what's happening in today's digital living room.

Whether you want to call it interactivity, agency, autonomy or anything else, the most painfully obvious advancement is that games have taken us past passively watching television and reading books. You can watch a car chase on television, but it's kind of different when you're the one going 150 MPH and outrunning the cops in your red Ferrari. With games we're in the driver's seat.[12] That level of control changes things, making them look and feel different to the brain. The physical experience that gamers have comes close to matching what they get through reality.[13]

Games like chess, mah-jong, and dice gambling have been around for generations, and there's a reason that they're more fun to play than to watch. Being able to control the action places our minds into an arena where we can experiment and learn without some of the finality that we would get in real-world situations.[14] Many scholars have argued that playing games is a huge survival advantage for the humans and animals that play.[15] Stories on a television screen can inform us, but short of reality, a game is what *teaches*. Being able to see what happens when we make those dangerous choices, being able to then make our own spontaneous choices has made history's games inviting, exciting, and lasting. Playing might just be in our DNA.

Our science for creating better-quality games, or game design, has seen some major advances in the last hundred years; most notably in the 1950s. When those wily nerds started making complicated systems for play-fighting, they challenged young people to envision imaginative adventures—from swords and sorcery to spycraft and murder mystery. Early gamers would then take their heroes into these adventures, rolling dice in order to determine things like combat, or how much treasure they'd get. We eventually called these paper and dice games: gamers wrote down their hero's (or villain's) details on pieces of paper and most owned impressive inventories of dice. As it became ever more fun and easy to enter these different situations, we arrived at the notorious Dungeons & Dragons (D&D) franchise, which survives to this day. D&D's creators, Gary Gygax and Dave Arneson, both became proponents and icons for the gamer culture. In his book *Master of the Game*, Gygax wrote that the only valid purpose of gaming was to provide entertainment.[16] In the days of D&D, these strategic systems were so well refined that many of today's most advanced video games have changed them little. Some game developers abide fanatically by the actual Dungeons & Dragons rules.

In many ways games like D&D got people envisioning designs, but computers made this adventuring all the more easy. Computing power gave the game designers the blank slate that they needed for testing innovative ways to have these experiences. From Pong to Mario, every big advance in processing invited a new game designer to step in and wow us. Nowadays, with incredible computers and a massive backlog of old games, the game designers have innumerable tricks that they can use to make a game fulfilling. Where the designers once had to shape their imaginations to work around the technology, the technology has advanced to the point where it could work around imagination. Designers can re-create paper and dice systems or make shopping cart drag-racing games. Even though many contemporary game designers just replicate the game designs and themes that sell best, there's an incredible creative potential out there. The game that's been designed to be enjoyable is the first big advancement, or ingredient, that we refer to when we say "game" or "play." It's the experiential element, a technology that has enormous potential.

The second secret ingredient comes from a video game's social element. Games connect people. Gary Gygax wrote that without that connection, our experience of a game suffers: "...Its drama is less intense, its dangers abstract, its triumphs shallow." So imaginative minds took video games online. As early as the 1970s, designers built worlds purely out of text, worlds that could accommodate thousands.[17] Around the 1990s, we started getting big teams of people designing 3-D games, graphical systems that let up to a dozen or so people play cooperatively or competitively.

Then designers started to experiment with huge, visual online worlds. Today these are known as massively multiplayer online games, MMOs or MMORPGs for short. The story at the start of this section dealt with the MMO World of Warcraft. When thousands of people could come online and play together, these worlds really became a different kind of game. They were persistent, online most all of the time. Unlike a book, a flight of fancy that paints pictures in your head only so long as you read, these games had become a kind of place.[18] Like a 24-hour diner, you could stop by and have a sandwich, but the place doesn't open up or close down on anyone's schedule.

These persistent online places didn't have to be particularly well-designed; some were and are just big social spaces. Today these are worlds like Second Life or There.com; in the days of MUD games they were spaces like LambdaMOO. People in purely social worlds may not log on expecting the latest in graphics, or the most thrilling of game design. If they did, they'd probably come back to reality a little bit disappointed. We label these worlds "games" because they combine a persistent world with the 3-D visual graphics developed over the last decade, but there's a difference. Just having a persistent 3-D community isn't the same thing as having a pre-designed and satisfying game. You can walk and talk in most of these worlds, but they're a different technology; much more like a living room, a social experience rather than a kind of game system.

Other persistent worlds combine connectivity with game design. Mixing these two secret ingredients creates something strong. Once the designer makes our experiences inside a persistent world more game-like, more about the fun of playing, we start to see a space less about using these technologies to create an online living room. Instead, the other people are there to make the game seem more important. The Digital *Leveling* Room, consists of games like Ultima Online, Everquest, Star Wars Galaxies, Final Fantasy XI, and World of Warcraft that provide a social world that's also designed to make character progression rewarding. As gamers get the social status, skill levels, and swords that they need to play the game well, they're rewarded with increasing gratification and satisfaction. These games provide the best of both worlds — that feeling of stepping inside a lasting and populated space, but also heavy helpings of an entertaining game. It's like that 24-hour café from earlier, only it specializes in serving hot bliss. And this is a pretty cool way to advance the living room. Today's gamers enter the space, have a powerful experience, and their accomplishments *last*. What's more, those accomplishments are waiting patiently for gamers when they start their next gaming session, sometimes along with the other living people that they've been playing with. The digital leveling room is something new, a game which arguably causes the most problems for balancing reality and illusion.

As the look and feel of gaming changes, especially in the next few years, we're going to see some major changes in *where* gamers can play and *how* they do it. In the past they used chunky little controllers and bulky computers. Now computers are smaller, faster and in many more places; the face and physicality of gaming is already starting to change.[19] There are dancing pads which, in games like Dance Dance Revolution, make an entire game out of our footwork. The Nintendo Wii lets us swing a controller in order to simulate tennis, bowling and fishing. The Wii Fit adds a lot of the functionality you'd expect from dance pads. The next generation of games and gaming systems won't just connect us to friends around the world. More games are going to involve getting up and off of the couch.

And maybe even out of the house. In countries around the world, people interact and play in more places than just their living rooms; tomorrow's "living room" might stretch across many different kinds of places.[20] In Singapore, for instance, there's an entire industry that seems to be built around the concept of getting out of the house. Gamers convene at 24-hour shopping malls, 24-hour gaming cafes, but rarely, it seems, at home. In Seoul, the biggest city in South Korea, it's hard to find a single city block that doesn't have at least one PC room. Especially with denizens of the younger generation, these places are often packed full of people looking to talk with friends, play games, or to escape a cold and rainy night, even after every other social space has closed.[21]

While for many the living room has been a place of passively sucking down television, gaming will keep increasing our options. It already has for many, cutting across cultures in startling ways. For cultures that revolve around getting out of the house, gaming will follow the people.

Some whole countries already revolve around cell phones, using them as credit cards and book readers. Many of the bestselling books in Japan are downloaded and read on mobile phones.[22] No matter the country and no matter what we mean by "game," most people are looking to be entertained — which has until now been looked on as legitimate.

With gamers around the globe, one of the most interesting things to look at is how, and whether, they play socially. There's some question over the real level of connectivity between gamers who only know each other online. For players meeting in reality as well as online, especially in Asia, the cybercafé has become a kind of Mecca.

Though she's always been around video games, Canadian researcher Florence Chee says that she "never thought they would be anywhere near a career." The more that Chee saw gaming problems represented in the media, the more that she felt they were building up a kind of "myth of the addicted gamer." The word addiction was being bandied around in a way that she remembers as "all too cavalier for my liking." As she continued with her own research into games, however, she was inspired by the nuanced research produced by academics like T.L. Taylor and Ted Castronova.

She explains, "What they really did well was drive home the many facets of gaming in cultural and economic terms, lending insight to what was an obscure world rife with superstition and folklore such as 'One click and you're addicted.'"

That lead Florence to her own research, during which she remembers coming across stories of South Korean gamers and their reported notoriety for gaming addiction. Eager to know if the sensationalism was warranted, she took intensive language courses and saved for four months of field research.

Influences from our local cultures, according to Chee, are impossible to remove from the parts of our lives we spend in games. She emphasizes this by bringing up the writings of Clifford Geertz. "He asserts that beyond the brush strokes and the technical understanding of the form of art, one must understand the cultural context from which it emerges. An example he uses is that it is impossible to understand Arabic poetry (in Morocco) without understanding the Qur'an. That said, play is a part of culture, and the way people play is inextricable from their everyday life."

How different peoples live has far-reaching effects on how they play. One key example of this with game addiction is the line between work and leisure. "...The average South Korean works 2,390 hours each year, which is 34 percent more hours than the average in the United States." Contrasting America's more distinct notions of work and leisure, she notes that "the two categories seemed much more fluid in Korea."

In South Korea, at least 54 percent of the population, or 25 million people, play online games.[23] There, as with any country, culture has a deep effect not simply on any one sensational issue, but rather on how people play and what that means to them.

One major piece of the South Korean gamer culture is their unique cybercafé, the PC Baang — otherwise called a "PC Room" or a "PC Barn." In a recent conference panel, noted Korean judge Unggi Yoon spoke candidly about the emergence of the PC Baang.[24] During the Asian economic crisis, many laid-off workers began creating and populating these PC Baangs, creating a cheap and accessible kind of social space. Older games, most especially StarCraft, first released in 1998, and both Lineage I and II, developed as prominent games alongside the Baang. The games and Baangs also grew alongside Korean notions on what group cohesion and skill meant in relation to games. As stated by Judge Yoon, "The purpose of Lineage was not to kill, but to belong."[25]

In her fieldwork, Florence Chee noted that players continually mentioned something called Wang-tta, a concept which seemed to apply both to individual gamers and the larger groups inside the Baang; if a gamer's skills began to slip, or if they rejected gaming altogether, then they could be mocked and bullied, even ostracized. I have observed similar sentiments in other Southeast Asian countries, most notably in Malaysia and Singapore; there were reports that a lack of skill could spark real fistfights. To the person in the fistfight, often what's happening is taken for granted. Some of these gamers might not really see why a notion like Wang-tta stands out, but as the saying goes, a fish probably doesn't know that he's in water. Situations like this show why culture is key.

Korea might not just be an interesting case study, though. Being on the cutting edge of digital society, South Korean citizens may be chief innovators behind the cultural mores, laws, features and overall direction in which gaming takes the whole of the world. South Korea has already begun the tricky business of regulating online spaces, having for instance made it illegal to profit from something called botting. Try asking your local lawmakers for their stances on botting. Because these emergent types of cases can set a precedent for other countries, the legal cases and rulings in Korea could have a *major* influence on how we come to regulate a technology that crosses borders constantly.

Korea has also been on the forefront of tackling game addiction, which currently has their Ministry of Health in a state of emergency. They estimate that anywhere between two and three million youth in Korea are addicted, and have actually created government funded boot camps for re-training the very young. The *New York Times* recently researched these facilities, which have four times as many parents volunteering their middle-school aged children than there were spaces for them. There are instant help hotlines available for people to call for counseling, and Korea has also created the first fully unique diagnostic for detecting addiction, completely tailored to their culture. Unlike the first diagnostics and checklists to come out in the USA, discussed later, the Korean K-Scale is reported to reflect the actual problem far better. Overall, Korea gives us some great examples of how specific pieces of culture can lead gamers to play in certain ways.

Though culture's actual influence tends to be more subtle, there are a few other powerful things occurring worldwide that serve as unique examples. One of the most striking occurs when children, most especially boys, "fail to launch." That is to say that more often, and for a variety of reasons, children are living with their parents long after they've completed a basic high school education. These young adults, not seeking education, employment or training, NEET for short, are sometimes considered at risk for withdrawing from society. This isn't always a cause for concern in some countries, Italy, for instance. Parents have historically expected children, even young married couples, to live at home for some time, though they tend to do so while working and carrying on a full life. In many cases worldwide, these young people are closeting themselves away, sometimes living for decades in seclusion.

The most notorious case comes from the Hikikomori of Japan, where there's a growing stigma of young people who live primarily on their parents' income. This issue is actually fairly complex, having economic, social, and psychological components unique to Japanese culture. While it's plain to see that a Hikikomori living at home would have greater access to something like games, we should see it as just one more example to how unique cultures open up unique windows to play. These different motivators don't usually tie directly into addiction; they don't uniquely cause the gaming problem, but rather provide us with reasons, ways and means to play.

In many ways, beyond just gaming, technology is changing what it means to live, love and have fun in a global information age. Some of the namecalling and finger-pointing in game addiction is just a continued failure to understand technological innovation. In other cases, addictions can by fueled by a failing to understand gaming and the ways culture can push someone to excess play. These problems are new; they're emergent in ways, cultural or not, that haven't been given enough credit.

There's usually a lot happening when the secret ingredients, interactivity and connectivity, take over someone's life. It's not just C'thun's evil gaze, or the banter that we get with our living companions behind the screen. The digital living room gives us more than just tangible goals. From how these goals are structured, to how our physical bodies get yanked in, the gaming experience pulls on most gamers for reasons that few can put their fingers on. On the one hand, some of the magic comes from not being able to see the man behind the curtain. On the other, the proverbial wizard behind everything isn't going to pop out and force you to take care of your life. Sometimes he'll let the show drag on for a very long time.

It shouldn't be entirely surprising when games fall out of balance, especially when powerful reasons to play are combined with the almost undeniable feeling that what gamers are experiencing is real. A gamer's brain and body are getting an overflow of mixed messages; real-feeling experiences mix with legitimate reasons to play, making problems hard to perceive or accept. The danger is that where a gamer sees only fun, friends and good times, their real lives could be collapsing around them. If things in reality do implode, then often this leaves them with a distracting alternative: a powerfully satisfying though semi-real world. But will games lure in and lock in every last one of us?

No Escape

"It took me a long time to learn how to move around," says Dr. Angeline Khoo, recounting her first time in an MMORPG. "It seems so silly now."

When I first met Dr. Khoo, she struck me as the kind of university professor who makes college worth the tuition. With a desire to go beyond just the "games are evil" mentality of the late nineties, she stepped outside her comfort zone. She took the time to play.

Khoo first got into games "without having any intention of staying too long." But, she recalls, "I got hooked! I am still very much in the game!" Though Angeline has spent the past 18 years teaching at Singapore's National Institute of Education, one can get the feeling that getting into these games was no easier for her than it would have been for my own mom. Though in the game, dark corners and oversized spiders frightened her at first, Khoo faced her fears, ultimately using her experiences in-game to make serious contributions to the research available. More importantly, she has proven that sophisticated games aren't out of reach for everyday folks. Having played them, she sees a bright future for games. At the same time she's become more acutely aware of the challenges.

"The game world can be both exciting and a warm social environment, but because it is so it becomes hard to leave it for a more stressful and mundane world outside," says Dr. Khoo. "Hence, excessive play and time management is a challenge — for most, if not all players."

But does this mean that we have to discount video games altogether? Is it bad that this up-and-coming living room invests and involves us in empathy for total strangers? Dr. Khoo doesn't think so. With a grin, she recounts trading turkey recipes, mentoring young gamers, and learning more about people from across the globe, most especially through quirky cultural exchanges.

"Recently, I learned about what people do on Thanksgiving," she says. In having these unique cultural moments, games bring us together. Khoo, who is of Chinese ancestry, remembers discovering surprising cultural similarities. "I would cook and freeze food for my husband when I have to go overseas — I found that one of my guildmate's wives does same thing for him — and he's in Tennessee."

In the end, what strikes me about Dr. Khoo is how deeply she's been affected by the people playing online. She sums it up simply, "I've made a lot of friends whom I have come to care a lot for."

No matter whom you talk to or where in the world they come from, bonds are being formed in today's digital living room. New people are learning to act and interact inside, while newer living rooms and leveling rooms are being made easier to understand. It's happening right now, as you read these very words. Some players aren't going to want to leave these screens. It's not that everyone is going to transform on the full moon and begin hungering for these online coffee shops and digital diners. As popular media technologies start to change, some of these game worlds could easily become the next step in popular services like digital cable; by and large current consumers will pay their money and upgrade. Entering the digital living room should be as simple as sitting in your real one.

Technologies that have been around all along are already changing for us. These changes are giving us more say in what we read, watch and listen to; the alchemists behind the scenes and screens are designing those choices to be fun, and in some cases to connect us with one another. It's happening right now, and people have, by and large, been eating it up. The secret ingredients are hard to resist. We aren't playing with improved television, digital books or online games because they're addictive, at least not yet. Everyday people play along because they're getting more of the entertainment that they want.

This new breed of entertainment is also profitable to the point of absurdity. Blizzard Entertainment, developer of the popular American MMO World of Warcraft, generates annual revenues *exceeding* one billion U.S. dollars from the single game. Warcraft has over eleven million active players and was probably the key motivator behind an 18.9 billion-dollar merger between parent company Vivendi and Activision.[26] It's hard to imagine one game being worth all that. As of our writing, the makers of Asia's most popular online world MapleStory have boasted that over fifty million people have active accounts.[27] Tens, if not hundreds of millions of real human beings actively play inside these places. There's too much money to be made for developers to *not* aggressively expand into newer markets. If you haven't gotten into gaming yet, then it probably won't be long before all of the fun, interactivity, and connectedness of these worlds eases on into your life.

It also won't hurt that we'll be able to hop inside from anywhere on Earth. As handheld, wireless-internet computers become more prominent, devices like the iPhone, some people can already step inside parts and parcels of the digital living room from wherever they want. As smaller computers combine with evermore universal wireless internet, the knowledge of how to make compelling games will be used to make worlds accessible from practically anywhere people would want to play.[28]

New e-book readers like Amazon.com's Kindle already do that, only for books. They use a wireless internet network to transmit books to a handheld reader. With different technologies, including a six-inch "electronic paper" material, the part of the living room that deals with reading has already gone digital. We can buy and browse articles, magazines and novels, all using one single handheld tablet.[29] Even though Kindle is adding versatility only to the written word, gamey social worlds started out as "just text." If it were possible to play today's games on the bus, some people wouldn't look away from their monitors for anything.

These "games" are so important to some people, even now, that professionals in a few different industries have started to use them as a place to meet and play with business partners and colleagues. Being plugged into them may fast become just as professionally important to some people as checking email, reading industry news, or even *doing* their work. To quote an older saying, mostly used by professionals already in tech industries, "*World of Warcraft* is the new golf."[30] A number of entrepreneurs are counting on businesses to encourage this type of play, early worlds having already been hatched to connect and train different types of professionals.[31]

This living room is one that's unafraid of change. You might think that online business meetings are uncomfortable, but only so long as you keep doing them while wearing all of your stuffy business clothes. In situations where hours of traffic, government restrictions, or even an ocean might otherwise keep homesick people from seeing loved ones on Thanksgiving, some families choose to meet in *Guild Wars*, one of those dark and nefarious MMO games. Even though these places are but the lovechildren of games and the internet, they're becoming more than just entertainment.

The images on the screen can sometimes be more than just illusion. Once these technologies give everybody a window into the living room of their friends and families, balancing digital living with physical living will be an issue. The technology that puts people's faces onto a television in real time, which you could loosely call "telepresence," will almost definitely be a standard home appliance before long.[32] Today's gamers have to wrap their minds around the idea of presence right now. Games pull the curtains of a window, one which lets you and your friend look inside the same illusionary world together. Each of you then plays the puppeteer, controlling the detailed and intricate movements that go into the business of dragon-slaying. Or spaceship construction. When just anyone is given the ability to look in, puppets or not, some everyday folks will have problems with balance.

As far as artistic expression goes, game design is still a long way from mature. We've done a lot of really neat things, but even games that *look* radically different will often use tired concepts that date back at least to D&D (for instance, "hit points" and "random damage"). The storytelling isn't much better. Plot in most games rarely attempts to go beyond "You are a gun-toting space marine. Kill everything." We have games that let players control gun-toting space marines from a first-person perspective, games with gun-toting space marines in a top-down perspective, and games where gun-toting space marines race each other in Humvees. A lot of normal people like movies like *Predator, Starship Troopers,* and *Aliens.* Other people enjoy romance movies like *Love Actually* or *Bridget Jones' Diary,* long dramas like *Dances with Wolves,* even beautifully constructed and artistic movies like the *Pillow Book* or *Wings of Desire.* Right now an Xbox, PlayStation or Nintendo puts games on a television, but that's not enough. People watch movies or play games because the themes make sense to them on a personal level. Before games can hit the mainstream, they're also going to have to be meaningful for *everyone.*

In the end, we're going to embrace games because of what's really engaging in the digital living room: themes that speak to us and designs that get our hands on the secret ingredients. It's not going to be because games are instantaneously addictive or purposefully nefarious. The bad play only starts to grow when people jump into gaming without understanding the game or themselves. When that kind of a player goes nuts, then at some point they'll only ever want the joy of swords and sorcery — not the moderately rewarding life which feeds their living organs. A responsible player, today or tomorrow, will understand how games work, plan ahead, and stay balanced.

The power of any story has been its ability to show us how we might make a better reality. Fantasy helps us to see the world through reinvigorated eyes; imagination takes us beyond the status quo.[33] If playing in a game helps us to improve our real lives, then that's all we can ask for. What media isn't supposed to do is replace a life. The line between reality and illusion is complicated and subtle, but it's one that many more of us will be walking soon. Understanding this line begins with what is arguably the most important puzzle piece: how our physical bodies see and hear what's happening in the digital living room.

Two

MEDIA EXPERIENCE AND REAL ILLUSION

Hamlet, Prince of Denmark ... has excited questions about its meanings over centuries, and in many languages.... It has grown a literature of tens of thousands of learned papers and books of comment, and at least one journal.... We speak of Hamlet as thinking ... Hamlet as being conscious. But Hamlet never lived. He is but a product of the bard's wonderful imagination.[1] — R.L. Gregory

Shakespeare's *Hamlet*, though only a story, has enchanted millions. In spite of being completely fictional, most of the stories that we tell play a huge role in helping us to understand our universe, our world, even ourselves. We live and breathe them, yet very few people understand what actually happens in our brains and bodies when we read a play, listen to the radio, or watch a movie. These media are all livable and breathable stories; they each excite different senses, senses which employ unique methods for pulling the human mind into worlds.

When it comes to engaging the brain, video games blow them all away. Games take players inside, *immersing* them by portraying fantastic and imaginative worlds, believable visual imagery, and interactivity that they can't help but pay attention to. Some games take it a step further and connect players to other real people. Depending on what's responsible for the immersion, the human body can release a variety of chemicals, responding to games as though they were a completely real, physical experience.

It's easy for some people to hate games. This book is, after all, about people who can't stop playing. While the immersions in games do present us with new and serious challenges, games are simply the state of the art in a long tradition of storytelling. That storytelling is what builds up our ability to live in a society — whether it's the jungles of Papua New Guinea or the urban jungle of Los Angeles, whether we learn from a book or a game. This chapter isn't just about understanding games; it's about understanding your world. For that, we have to start this story at the beginning.

Worlds Without Words

> Human beings are unique to other species in that we live in a world that is created by the stories we tell. Most of what we know, or think we know, we have never personally experienced; we learned about it through stories.[2] — George Gerbner

Writing turns us into time-traveling explorers. Whether someone has chiseled symbols into clay tablets or accidentally clicked "reply all" on an email, writing down our thoughts often gives then unexpected mileage. Because humans have invested so much time and effort into improving the ability to share stories and experiences, written words can transcend space and time. Though our storytelling ability is one that the species can both love *and* hate, it's an ability that people *rarely* go without. It's the basis for history, literature, cinema, and on some levels even culture and civilization. Without a way to illuminate the minute details of your life, without technologies like language, photographs and email, we just wouldn't know how to act in society as we know it. There wouldn't *be* society as we know it.

Today, people use dozens of different technologies in order to share their stories and experiences. When we use things like language, television and video games, we're going beyond what we could have experienced with our own senses. We're using these media to have some kind of experience. Whether it's talking on a cell phone so that we can experience the voice of a friend, or reading a book so that we can experience some kind of story, these *media experiences* are advancing like never before. Video games might seem outrageous and new. Though they're fundamentally different from books, radio, even television and movies, games are also the natural progression of these technologies. They're the most sophisticated form of storytelling, or more accurately, media experience, available to a general public.

Games do seem to be poking our brains in ways that are keeping gamers sitting in front of their screens.[3] There are primitive pieces to our brain, and not all of them ask permission before stealing us away into fantasy worlds.[4] Knowing how this media experience works, from its history to its foundations in the human brain, will help you to actually understand why games pull people in, beyond just the mystical word "addiction." Knowing how media experience works is handy knowledge in a world of 24-hour cable news, flying advertisements, and real-world presidents giving campaign speeches inside the digital living room. Before we get into how these technologies work, we've got to talk about where they started.

For untold years, let's just say millions of them, our ancestors have been using physical hardware (like eyes and ears) to have their own little *personal* experiences. If these ancestors ate a yummy yellow banana, then they might have remembered, or at least recognized, that yellow equals yummy. If they can also manage to remember where they found the banana, that's not too shabby. Knowing how to find good food increases one's chances for survival, right? Say this ancestor of ours watches a friend, Ooki, eat a red banana. Although seemingly very delicious, it kills Ooki almost instantly. Sorry, Ooki. If our ancestor can remember this experience, then he can avoid instantaneous red banana death.

Just remembering often isn't enough. We have to protect the tribe, right? If the ancestor has some way of sharing Ooki's untimely demise with others, then they could also avoid the red bananas, maybe even destroy them. Whether by making crazy gestures at the red banana, or calmly saying, "Hello my tribe, eating this banana *will kill you*," capturing our own experience via some media technology, even language, is allowing others to experience something outside of themselves. They didn't watch Ooki die, but now they understand that our ancestor did. More importantly, they know not to eat the banana.

Within the last few thousand years, we've started to wildly advance technologies for capturing experience. From alphabets to paintings, these new technologies allow us to share experiences of things we've done, stories we've heard, and products of our own imaginative fancies. These technologies serve as the only verifiable way to understand our past, as our memory of history lasts only as long as its record. Historian Thomas Cahill reflects the sentiment of many historians, saying, "If there are no books, there's no civilization."[5] There are many theories on how we developed writing. One is that it originated with the Phoenicians, around the edges of the Mediterranean Sea. Others point to the Sumerians, who may have had whole libraries of inscribed tablets as far back as 3000 B.C.[6] Wherever the written word began, in time we've developed thousands of languages and many different technologies for passing on experiences; each technology uses different physical senses and different combinations of senses. These technologies allow others to see or imagine an experience that was not their own. They have a "media experience" and are taken beyond what they alone have personally experienced.

Books and writing can transport that experience over great distances, but often they will also cause the writing to outlive the writer. For example, even if this book were published yesterday, I may have written these words ten years ago. As far as you know, I might be dead. Some technologies amplify speaking and writing. Radio makes it possible for one person to fire their voice into the air, sometimes talking to millions of people simultaneously, sometimes to people on the other side of the planet. Printing presses allow many identical books, making them cheaper and vastly more available. Photographs and paintings allowed the sharing of *images*. Video cameras allowed still photographs or paintings to evolve into motion. Where at first we could only *describe* stories and experiences to someone, later we could *show* them.

Games now allow us to *live* them. We experience events firsthand. Some games place players into deep stories with emotional involvement; others present players with interesting or engaging experiences (sometimes divorced from story, background and reality altogether). Like many media experiences, games are a man-made technology that has to come from outside our bodies. Unlike spoken language, books, or even movies, games aren't just describing or presenting an experience. Games *are* experience. Instead of seeing, hearing, or imagining a situation, game players interact with that situation, and this advance has opened the door to a revolution which has only just begun.

As games continually set the bar higher for the technology of experience, they make traditional problems more pronounced. Ever wonder why looking away from the television can be so hard for some people? Academic Ann Marie Barry has. She asserts, "Because evolution is a slow process, our brains have not yet adapted to visual experience gained via media in any special way.... For the brain's perceptual system, visual experience in the form of the fine arts, mass media, virtual reality, or even video games is merely a new stimulus entering the same prewired circuits ... and is processed in the same way."[6]

Games are incredibly effective at tricking our eyes, and that's only one of the many problems not being talked about. Though the media we consume presents certain problems, especially in video games, media experience is not just about games. Religion, celebrity gossip television, education — they all rely on the technologies of media experience. Even though gaming is creating wholly new branches in the media experience tree, it also has deep roots in these other technologies. Humans have been building up the ability to showcase experiences for thousands of years, and for good reason. Without media experience we can't share or preserve our thoughts on what it means to be human. Considering that, it shouldn't surprise us that the art of illusion is perhaps one of the most celebrated and honored pursuits in human history.

Immersed in Imagination

"They say he raped them that night," writes Julian Dibbell. His book *My Tiny Life* is still considered by many game designers and scholars to be one of the most pointed and relevant tours of the gaming world.[8] It was based upon the following story, which originally ran in a 1993 edition of the *Village Voice*.[9] Dibbell's rape doesn't happen outside a café, in some college dorm, or a shadowy parking lot. It happened in LambdaMOO, a "rustic mansion built entirely of words." *My Tiny Life* describes a version of the digital living room that's been built entirely out of text.

"They say that ... he forced them to have sex with him, and with each other and to do horrible, brutal things to their own bodies ... it all happened in the living room — right there amid the well-stocked bookcases and the sofas and the fireplace — of a house I came later to think of as my second home."

The brutish villain of this story is Mr. Bungle, the "bisquick-faced clown," who was "girdled with a mistletoe-and-hemlock belt." He attacked them in the living room — the place inside LambdaMOO where they felt the safest.

Mr. Bungle first forced one male character to copulate him in various ways. He then forced others to have sex with each other. Even after being ejected from the living room, he raped them from afar. Using only graphic description, he violated other players in ways that they would have never anticipated.

Stories, good or evil, have the capacity to capture us. To carry us away. When we're young, even the simplest of bedtime stories can capture us, pull us in, and transport us to other worlds: *Where the Wild Things Are* or *Harry Potter*'s Hogwarts, for example, not to mention the places we'd go with Dr. Seuss. Kids can be insatiable, demanding that their parents read their favorite tales again and again. They might cherish the drawn pictures, the story's detail, the sound of the reader's voice, or sometimes all of the above. J.R.R. Tolkien, writer of *The Lord of the Rings*, and *The Hobbit*, suggested over 50 years ago that great works of fantasy create secondary worlds which the human mind could step inside and believe. By the power of words alone, we sometimes leave the primary world; that world where right now you're having an experience of this book.[10] We enter a world that exists wholly in our own minds. This concept has profound meaning for the good and bad in media, whether we're talking about radio, television, or games.

Reading a story out of a newspaper, like most of the stories we'd hear on a regular basis, normally doesn't take us from the everyday, humdrum world. The kind of escape that Tolkien is talking about is rare. There are amazing stories out there, but the way in which brains physically process grammar and words makes it harder for us to fall into worlds made just out of words.[11] That doesn't mean that novels are subservient to movies. It means that immersion into the fictional world is less automatic for human hardware. In many cases (some would argue most), books can be vastly more dynamic and colorful than the best games. Literature, given the chance to start fermenting in our minds, can carry us off.

Purely from a biological standpoint, the processing of words is less immediate and less instinctive than seeing.[12] Humans process sight very quickly, and language is often divorced from other senses. During regular experience, when we're off in the real world doing our thing, certain kinds of sensations get sent to different parts of our brains, what one Harvard professor, Steven Pinker, has called modules. In his book *How the Mind Works*, Pinker notes that the sections in our brain where we process sight and language are necessarily separate.[13] Text is largely interpreted in the relatively advanced prefrontal cortex. While this is an area in the brain responsible for higher thought, it isn't the part of the brain that's going to let us have visceral, emotional and automatic responses.

Many prominent neuroscientists agree. Antonio Damasio, considered to be one of the world's leading experts on the human brain, has said that language processing necessarily happens separate from processes like sight.[14] When speaking with a friend, you might see their facial expressions, hear their words and also understand the deeper meanings of what they're saying. Things flow naturally. However as Keith Kenney, a scholar in visual communications put it, "In effect, it is a trick of timing." The brain puts those sensations together for us.[15]

Whatever the brain does, it tends to do a good job. On a practical level, speech, image, and imagination work together without much fuss. Sitting down to read we can "see" what's happening in a book. In the magic of media experience, people, places, sights and even smells can feel so real as to be utterly convincing. Your mind can almost leave your reality in order to enter one created with a paper and pen, or typewriter, or laptop. The mind falls into a secondary world. Tolkien called a complete immersion into a secondary world enchantment, saying that while not a dream, enchantment allowed one to wholly enter into "a dream that another mind is weaving."[54]

There is also something magical, almost sacramental, happening when someone is able to create one of these worlds. When one creates a world that another living human can enter, Tolkien saw that as following in the footsteps of some greater creator. "...We may cause woods to spring with silver leaves and rams to wear fleeces of gold, and put hot fire into the belly of the cold worm. But in such 'fantasy,' as it is called, new form is made; Faerie begins; Man becomes a sub-creator." Regardless of your spiritual or religious affiliation, Tolkien was right to name sub-creation as a unique force.

Tolkien was deeply critical of the phrase *willing suspension of disbelief*, the idea that readers must force themselves to believe what's happening in a story.[17] In his mind, much of reading's pleasure came from falling into a secondary world, not from forcing oneself to ignore the real world. If you've ever sat in a theatre that had a crying baby, then you'd know that suspension primarily only has to happen when you're being constantly interrupted. And good stories don't interrupt you. During pleasurable reading, watching of film and playing of games, we are unaware that anything beside the story or experience is occurring. There's a term that gamers use, as a way of saying how deeply they've been pulled into a game. They call it immersion, though an exact definition to the word has eluded nerds for decades. There are a number of ways in which gaming can immerse, and Tolkien's idea of enchantment is interesting in that it requires a little something extra: the artist.

Our brains don't make it easy to get immersed through words alone. Tolkien understood this, and said that for real enchantment to take place, something happened that went above and beyond mere writing. To Tolkien, sub-creation, this ability to craft convincing worlds, was *literally* magical. Only the deepest and most inspired artistic commitment, on the part of the writer, would be able to pull a person into an imagined world. People respond to creativity. It's refreshing to hear amazing stories of witches and wizards, wish-granting genies, and highly improbable space whales. Certain imagery engages our brains. Artistry, in word or picture, can immerse us. It casts a spell on us.

If a story lacks that artistry, or if something in the primary world is dragging you away, then the spell may be (at least momentarily) broken. If we finish a story and are satisfied, get too aggravated with it, or for some reason just give up on reading it, then we might call this disenchantment. You're no longer immersed in the secondary world. We usually aren't either completely enchanted or disenchanted with fiction, but rather somewhere in-between.

While books aren't the most direct way to get our experience, for centuries writers have been making worlds from words — without moving images, without computers, without sound. Words, whatever their disadvantages may be, can still fully draw us into an experience. They can both teach us philosophy and present us with riveting battles. The visual elements of television and video games, especially those with at least some splash of artistry, may have powerful advantages. Having a visual experience, like seeing some guy give an old lady "the finger," is transmitted and understood quickly. Though reading the description may evoke vivid imagery, it's not quite so instantaneous. Nor will you necessarily have the same response. Comprehending language physically takes the brain more time than the much more direct processing of vision. Maybe that's why Tolkien said that an enchanted story could produce fantasy with "realism and immediacy beyond the compass of any human mechanism," but that he had never seen such a thing done with success.

Human mechanism has changed.

Seeing Is Believing

> What is the use of a book, without pictures or conversations? —*Alice's Adventures in Wonderland*

While some words may be able to trick the senses, images are almost always far more automatic. In fact, when technology helps to realistically portray an enchanting story, the media experience stands a far greater chance of hooking us. Because the human eye lacks any inborn mechanism for separating the visual stimulus of real experiences from that of media experiences, imagery alone is very often enough to pull somebody in.[18] To better understand this, try imagining that you have never, *ever* looked at yourself in a mirror before. If you had no education of what was happening, that the mirror showed your reflection, then how long do you think it would take for you to grasp its mechanics? Humans, great apes, bottlenose dolphins and elephants are the handful of creatures that we know of who can actually learn to recognize themselves in the presence of a mirror.[19] Though it's hard to expect the process of learning to "use" a mirror to take long, humans and creatures have varying levels of maturity and wisdom. Sight, understanding, and then a spontaneous knowing, or belief in the image's fidelity — can it all happen at once or does it take time?

Once you understand the concept of a mirror, that it just lets you see yourself, what are you actually focusing on when you go to use one? Once the experience of seeing "you" is no longer novel, what's going through your mind? Is your focus more likely to be that you're looking at a reflected image on a reflective pane, or that you've got a mysterious ketchup stain on your shirt? For most experienced mirror users it's the ketchup. Our brains process images in a very basic and specific way; deep down the brain doesn't usually pause to distinguish between everyday, real images and those that we see in the mirror, on the television, or within a video game.

"But hold up a second!" You might be saying. "I know that TV isn't real! Why, even that reality TV stuff is staged!"

That's true, *you* might know that the images aren't real; it's that your eyes and brain don't have any mechanical way to differentiate. "Even in a life-long couch potato," writes Steven Pinker, "the visual system never 'learns' that television is a pane of glowing phosphor dots, and the person never loses the illusion that there is a world behind the pane."[20] Humans can't tell the difference between real sight and images on a television or computer screen. If somebody were to experience media visually, then certain parts of his or her brain will interpret what's seen as the genuine article. One scholar writes that the tricks are more played on the eye, less on the brain. "Pictures give us the false perceptual belief we are in the presence of the subject."[21] While that's not the whole story, there are many reasons that our perceptual system cannot tell the difference between *real* visual experience and experience got through certain forms of *media*, stuff like photographs in a newspaper, images on television, or objects in a video game. When our brains react to media as though it were real, this creates a kind of visual immersion that can single-handedly keep us playing.

Once the eye sees and passes along an image, that image hits specific areas inside the brain in a set order. That ordering is important, and it starts with the eyes. They actively scan what's around us, constantly sending images to the brain. To put this process simply, these images get split into two signals and sent over two pathways. The first has been called "quick and dirty," because it *very quickly* sends *very basic* shapes to the deeply emotional part of our brain: the amygdala. There, these basic shapes are compared against other known shapes stored in our emotional memory. Almost immediately, an emotional reaction is sent out.[22]

The slower of the two signals heads to the cortex, that thinking part of our brain. There we can first begin to realize what it is that we're seeing. Unfortunately, say many neuroscientists, thinking about images is so slow that before we even get a chance to think, we've already had a response. Say we're watching a zombie movie, and one gruesome fellow lunges at the camera, hungry for brains! Before we can say to ourselves, "Zombies aren't real. I still have my brains," our emotions have already screamed, "*Aiee! My brains!*" If you happen to jump so high that your companion gives a chuckle, then politely explain that your finely tuned reflexes will ensure your survival were this an actual zombie assault. Otherwise, be comforted that things just happen too fast with visual imagery. The immersion often can't be anything other than natural.

With no actual, mechanical chunk of brain or eye to remind us that we're having a media experience, visuals grant license to enter and exit secondary worlds with far more ease and fluidity. We may not actually speak with, shoot at or otherwise choose our own adventures with characters from our favorite shows. What we can do is learn to enter and enjoy the experiences presented to us. Thinking about it rationally we know that television shows aren't real. What happens on television stays on television. The problem is that brains aren't rational. The eye doesn't differentiate reality from illusion, and the brain doesn't do anything to help—at least, not while it's being held in thrall by fetching imagery.[23] On some level, anybody who sits down to play a game with visual elements is going to experience that game with the human eye, which doesn't possess any active mechanism for distinguishing between real life and visual media. Though we often think about what we've played after we've played it, that's not automatic. Visually, images seem to have the ability to immerse and enchant us—with or without our permission.

This sense stimulation is something that isn't recognized by some game designers. A book written by modern-day game designers Eric Zimmerman and Katie Salen says that complete immersion has to be forced.[24] "Players always know that they are playing," they write, insisting that the player has to work hard to suspend their disbelief. To these two popular authors, these distractions and abstractions make it impossible to ever enter something like a secondary world. And games most certainly throw up hurdles to immersion. Let's take a few pages to look at possible problems to a Tolkienesque kind of "enchantment," especially through the key arguments raised by Zimmerman and Salen.

In his visits to the local zoo, famous thinker Gregory Bateson observed that monkeys seemed to know the difference between "play fighting" and the real thing. While playing, dogs, monkeys and humans don't just nip, bite or punch, respectively. They also have an extra kind of language, subtle little hints which basically also say "we're not fighting." It's what he calls metacommunication.[25] Though a big word, this is an easy concept. Metacommunication really means that two or more people are sending each other small cues. These cues just hint at the bigger picture. So a man might be fighting with somebody, but sometimes he's also making other gestures that show his sparring partner that it's "just a game." Alternatively, that big-picture communication could be saying, "This isn't a game; I'm here to kill you." Our pugilists might go through the motions of having a fistfight, but there are small cues that tell whether they're being serious or silly.

To Salen and Zimmerman, even the act of turning on the game implies metacommunication; we always know that "it's only a game — because it isn't real." That makes sense on a cognitive level; media experience performed on a computer is not occurring in the primary world, in "real life," as it were. The argument here is that sitting at the computer is a type of tacit acknowledgement. "It," whatever our play experience may be, could be dropping nuclear bombs on peasants, or it could be mangling other real live people. It's true that we're not doing these things in reality, though it also seems that within interactive secondary worlds our brains would take most game experiences at face value. These are experiences, often with people and inside believable spaces.

Recall how humans deal with mirrors. When we turn on the bathroom light and look into one, it's most common to see a ketchup stain, or a ghastly zit, or ourselves. If the mirror is dirty, distorted, or on the ceiling, then we're going to have an irritating reminder that "it's only a reflection." In the same way, a dirty computer monitor, a badly designed game, or a malfunctioning mouse will to serve as a constant reminder that it's "just a game;" a constant reminder that there's more to the media experience. Otherwise our eyes are more inclined to automatically look past the computer monitor and into the game itself. We see lasers, or dragons, or whatever we happen to be experiencing inside the world. More than that, we're focused on avoiding the dragon breath or killer laser burns. Even the digital living rooms made entirely out of words get us looking past just a monitor. During the rape in LambdaMOO, there was certainly meta-communication. It's just that the message being communicated wasn't "It's no big deal, this is just a game." Real barriers of security and trust were shattered. Forced sex was the message, "whether you want it or not."

Looking through the monitor and into a world isn't the same thing as giving someone little cues that you're "just playing." A lot of the games out there don't even let you play with other people. So long as immersion holds, all of our communicating has to do with us, our personal experience of the game world. We tend to shift our attention to the primary world only when the game gets turned off or interrupted. When we do take a moment to step back, we can then make sense of what just happened in a secondary world. We might think, "OK, I didn't actually destroy that galaxy, I was just playing." With most games, though, we're usually too busy doing the destroying to exit the immediacy of the media experience.

Similarly, Zimmerman and Salen wrote that the little hints that "it's just a game" will always act as a nagging reminder that we're playing the game.[26] As we play, what we see is "...on a computer, in an operating system, in a browser, on a webpage, inside an interface...." A game's interface, or its different controls and framing, do sometimes take away from normal immersion. They cause problems when they're badly designed, inconsistent and glitchy. Good interfaces work just like the frame around a big, clean, and well-placed mirror. We look into the glass and interact with the image we see.

But even in the best games, disbelief is common when a game is unfamiliar. All players must contend with the learning curve of a new game. No matter the form it takes, *immersion must be learned*. For some media this can take a great deal of time, especially with those forms of immersion which are cognitive, more rooted in the thinking cortex. In secondary worlds, these are the ways of understanding and interacting that are deliberate, which have to be considered and planned. Other times the learning is instinctual, automatic and effortless, most especially when the experience being learned is more visual. Though, as even the most complex cognitive actions are repeated, or especially as they are more often associated with easily processed visuals, our ability to act and interact within the secondary world transforms, going from lumbering and clumsy to fluid and elegant.

The first time we type in a word processor or an excel spreadsheet, we must learn what it means to "save" our "file." One must ponder the action, perhaps click a few times before the action is complete. The more this cognitive action is performed, the more automatic it might become. As we learn, we associate saving files with a little blue disc symbol, the button that can be pushed in lieu of navigating menus. The more an automatic visual is incorporated, the more we learn to satisfy this desire to save a file through faster, easier, and more automatic means.

This kind of learning takes some people more time than others. My mother might go years without figuring out the meaning of common computer conventions like "CC," "reply all," and "paste." Games are unique in that it's one of their goals to make that learning process for each game as enjoyable as possible.[27] That said, processing critical thought and text does take our brains more time. In comparison, much less time has to be spent with visuals. This isn't to say that visuals never require extra training.

In television and cinema we deal with scenes being cut, dynamic editing, and avant-garde stylistic choices. Our brains must learn to interpret that. Only the most awful artsy films will overuse that form, making it impossible to understand what's going on. Learning to deal with media interfaces can at first be a distraction, but most humans quickly learn to process the abstraction. Without much effort they can have a media experience; they fall into the experience of what's being presented to them.

Whether it's television, games, or mirrors, humans of any culture don't simply learn these conventions; they learn to love the unique features of visual media. There are times where your intrepid narrator would have paid *good* money to be able to use Hollywood cutting conventions to fast-forward past a "long walking scene." Take a real-world example, the time that my friend Danny and I evaded a group of security guards by escaping into a dense bamboo forest. On the one hand, we two were glad not to be arrested. On the other, we had to hike through a dense bamboo forest. If you're thinking chirping birds, beautiful foliage, and the solitude of a seemingly ancient grove, then you've clearly not hiked through many dense bamboo forests. The two of us spent the next three hours in the dark and chilly shadows of the forest, squeezing between rock-hard pillars of live bamboo, negotiating impassable walls of dead gray bamboo, and walking through beefy spider webs, home to even beefier spiders. The idea of fast-forwarding through that experience still sounds nice. The point is that most of us don't just understand the idea of learned media conventions, in this case cutting scene. There are times when we humans would love it if life actually worked like that.

Abstractions in games can be similar. Take one of the most famous of the abstracted games: Tetris. You move blocks as fast as you can. If you get good enough at moving the blocks around, then you can move onto levels where your quick-block-moving ability is really put to the test. There are people whose block-moving skill is the stuff of legend, yet the look and the feel of Tetris is like nothing you're likely to have come across anywhere in nature. Humans can learn to manipulate this simple little game with alarming efficiency. In fact, this experience is something that we don't just learn to navigate, but our achievement inside the game is something that we can learn to crave just as much as being able to edit out our long bamboo forest escapade, or a miserable day at work. Whereas experiences in the primary world work in a fairly immutable way, secondary world experiences can be chosen. Gaming is a form of living where you often can use your favorite conventions, like cutting scene.

Sid Meyer's Civilization is another example of abstraction. In the game you lead a culture, say the Vikings or the Germans, through thousands of years of existence. You build cities, destroy cities, make war, make peace, tax your people, demand tribute from other peoples, make alliances, break alliances, impose social systems, ban social systems, launch nuclear weapons, ban nuclear weapons, and engage in a hundred other behaviors. All the while, this is your personal media experience. You must learn how each convention works inside the game, and your execution of these conventions either furthers or hurts your civilization. Learning the subtleties of the interface could take months, but truly dominating inside the world could take substantially more time. There's a learning curve in everything that we do in games. The contentions and conventions in games are designed to be fun to learn, but a joy to master.[28]

Immersion doesn't necessarily have to mean that we're becoming the character that we play. How much does somebody become their favorite television show host or comic book character? What immersion means (in adult humans with healthy brains, anyway) is that we see visual experience for what it is. If we're playing Halo, then we have an experience of actively shooting aliens. We live the action. If we watch a television action hero shoot some people, then that becomes a passive experience of just watching. Both can keep us watching, can immerse us purely through visuals. When you watch enough of one show, or read enough of a comic book, it can change how you react, your understanding of different situations. You might or might not approach them as a wiser person.[29] Experiencing something firsthand, as with a game, is no different. You don't become the hero or villain from your story, but you have been in their shoes nonetheless.

But notice that, whether the experience changes us or not, the chief concern is not *whether* the experiencer can descend into the experience. It seems rather to be *how deeply* they've entered. Most people aren't usually thinking about the mirror's frame while they're looking into it. The frame is ignored. They look at the mirror to see what's going on in the reflection. When we gaze past different frames, whether they sit around the edges of a mirror or a monitor, something magical *is* happening. Yet in neither a shooting game nor in the television show will a healthy human brain utterly and instantaneously *become* the persona inside the secondary world. Though players might enter and exit a game as their own complex selves, what more is the self but experiences? If a person has an experience presented to them long enough, who's to say that their brains won't ever change?

Even in games where we're actively trying to build a colorful character, becoming fully enchanted doesn't mean that we've become that character. In the normal course of learning to play, we might learn to act a different way inside a game, experiment with untested elements of our personalities, or play in the way that's most enjoyable, but we're always the ones playing. Becoming another person entirely is a mental disorder. Some gamers may play specifically so that they can role-play. That's more of what Bateson was talking about with metacommunication. If they have a healthy brain, then they'll always know who it is that they really are, and treating real people like garbage in a game is still treating real people like garbage. Some games might be well suited to a role-player's goals, but that player's visual experience of the world, and what his or her brain in turn processes and believes, is no different from any other healthy player's.

Since the work of sight mostly happens in the deeply emotional parts of our brain, games can sometimes call forth confusingly real sensations. While the brain may be separated into modules, it can be a well-integrated three-pound organ. Some memories are so holistic that if a video game presents us with the sights and sounds of a serene and windswept snow-filled valley, this may trigger physical feelings of cold, emotional nostalgia for the first time we saw real snow, human reflexes to snow, or all manner of odd and individualized reactions. Humans are, after all, odd and individualized creatures. We may only see a third-person view of a character, or an overhead view, but those images and thoughts can trigger connections stored deep in our emotional mind. The right stimuli inside a game might possibly call up smells, nostalgia for our first kiss, feelings of coldness, heat, dampness, and otherwise long-forgotten memories. And as we play, we add further layers of complexity to the emotional connections available inside secondary worlds.

Humans understand images implicitly. Though our minds can translate words into worlds, images breathe life into them instantly. Though we may know that we're just playing a game, our brains don't make that distinction automatically. We don't have to willfully suspend our disbelief, but rather suspend the belief that will has anything to do with it. Today's gaming experience is a lot like seeing ourselves in the mirror. At first, it might not be clear what exactly we're looking at. Unlike a completely baffled cat, hissing at the bizarro reflection cat, humans tend to figure it out pretty quickly. After that point, we can start to use the magic of the mirror automatically and tend to be able to use most any working mirror thereafter. While many games can pull us in via our different senses, there's another part of our brain which can be just as mischievous: the part that aims those sensations.

Divided Attentions

Have you ever tried reading a book while some blabbermouth just wouldn't stop taking? Especially when you only had a few pages left? There are reasons that this is so frustrating, reasons nestled in how humans actually pay attention to two things at once. William James was one of the first to start looking at how we divide our attentions, and he figured that we were able to split them. "Everyone knows what attention is," wrote James. "It implies withdrawal from some things in order to deal effectively with others...."[30] By his reasoning, we would give some attention to the insatiable talker and some to the book. The idea that attention could be split was the dominant thought on the issue for half a century. As it turns out, however, splitting attention doesn't work so well in the brain. The real inner workings of human attention are a major piece of the anatomy of both fun immersion and game addiction.

We need to be paying attention to something for it to make sense. When we multi-task, we're balancing our attention between two or more things. We're not actually "splitting" our attention, but rather we're *attention switching*; we are *quickly* switching the bulk of our focus from one thing to another. Some scientists have shown that we have a much harder time recalling things that we experienced while multi-tasking. When we multi-task, we store things in a part of the brain that's less effective at memory and more tailored to instinct. When we focus on one thing at a time, more of what we experience is processed in the comparatively advanced prefrontal cortex, which deals with some of the other higher brain functions that we've discussed, particularly with image and language.[31]

When more pointed research on attention began in the 1950's, it first focused on whether air traffic controllers would be able to hear two messages spoken at the same time. Experimenters played a different message in each ear. During the experiment, the listeners could understand the message coming into one ear, but recalled almost nothing about what was going into the other ear, besides the fact that there were sounds. The listeners' comprehension was so bad that they couldn't even tell when the words were being played backwards or when the messages were being spoken in another language! When the same messages were played with a delay of two to six seconds between each message, however, listeners were actually able to switch their attention back and forth, comprehending both.[32]

It turns out that our brains aren't just good at switching between conversations; they're also pretty good at figuring out what somebody is going to say next, especially since speech patterns in some languages and for some individuals are often predictable.[33] If what somebody will say is obvious enough, then our brains are likely to let us switch to a competing signal. If the brain expects more variation in what somebody is about to say, then we're more apt to listen closely. So, while we need to be paying attention to words if we want them to make sense, our brains do have some clever mechanisms for switching back and forth.

That said, it's clearly not impossible to do two things at once, especially when one of those tasks is automatic and single senses are being devoted to a single tasks. One of the best examples of this is driving with a cell phone. We don't literally go blind once we call up our best friend; it's just that we're switching our attention between the traffic and the talker. When the road gets particularly perilous, we're more likely to tune out the conversation so that we can avoid danger. We switch. The talking goes to the more automatic, the "autopilot." If we find out that our friend's father just passed away, we're more likely to tune out the road, giving sympathy to our friend. We switch back. The driving goes to the "autopilot." In that sympathy example, driving becomes a lot more dangerous because we're most likely relying only on our instinctual visual sense in order to pilot the vehicle. No matter how great and mighty someone's talking-while-driving skills may be, there will always be risk. Ironically, if we want to pay attention to the road, we're better off avoiding the juicier and more important cell phone calls while in the car. The ones that we really need to answer are more likely to distract us from being able to anticipate the flaming dumpster that's barreling towards our car.

Driving with distraction is a great way to introduce what's happening with gaming, because in both cases you can find various mixtures of sensations. You can engage the parts of your brain responsible for processing text, vision, and likely a few other sensations, all while sitting down. Paying attention to something means that it'll be mulled over alongside working memory, where the brain actually works to understand situations.[34] Stuff that we're not paying attention to just doesn't get the same level of service. If we're busy thinking about what's happening inside a game, then everything else is much more likely to fade away, or at least dim in comparison. In the long term, giving priority to a game means that we're not going to have any long-term memory for things that happened in the primary world.

So what, besides luck, can explain the people who seem to get away with not giving a road or a game their full attention? Perhaps that we're visual creatures, that our brains have a massive archive of very basic images, that having these tuned into our brain's reflex centers keeps us turning the steering wheel well enough. If we're used to a particular highway, or a particular type of game, or rather if we have enough muscle memory and visual experience, then it may be possible to "use the force," driving or playing by instinct.

It helps to explain those mysterious moments where zombie drivers arrive at a destination, with no memory whatsoever of having driven there. Players who re-enter the primary world with little memory of the game may have experienced a similar phenomenon; their minds may have known how to navigate the "roads." That said, driving with one's attention elsewhere seems incredibly dangerous. Such drivers and players will have moments where a mangy dog is going to jump out at them. The mangy dog, in other words something unexpected or startling, will force the brain to change the direction of a person's focus. By the time that happens, it could very well be too late to make meaningful corrections.

Thinking is just one more area where we can focus our attention. For instance, it's possible to be thinking about something so intently that you've no idea what somebody just said to you. Being lost in thought could be your reason for driving like a zombie. Your mind can wander its little heart out, and can become so scattered then you may have no recollection whatsoever of even what you were thinking about. Thinking can distract us from thinking. While the brain has neat ways of processing vision, words and thought, it's limited in how much attention it can shell out at once.

This helps us to understand why the game experience can be so involving. In the primary world, real things vie for our attentions — billboards, girlfriends, the subwoofers of other people's car stereos, you name it. We see them, we hear them, we think about them. Even though games might, at first glance, seem to be just one more distraction, they're more than that. Games are an entire world of distraction. Once the realistic game is turned on, there are attractive distractions that can keep your eyes from inaction. You see the images, often read text, and most importantly you're thinking about what's going on inside the game world. Because good games always have you looking for something, reading something, or thinking about something, it gets harder to switch your attention back onto reality.

People are giving secondary world events and distractions the same level of attention and feeling that they give to the most important life decisions in the primary. Sometimes more, since they're often filled with fast action and intrigue. While games might seem like they should only be one distraction, they are capable of dividing our attentions just as effectively as the real world, causing a very effective attentional immersion. Whether or not we're playing with anybody else, our minds are going inside.

Attention immersion is just as powerful as any other. When so many different flashy signals exist inside a secondary game world, it doesn't matter if it's visually realistic or groundbreakingly imaginative. It doesn't matter if you're moving small shapes, as in Tetris, or if you're wearing a dozen pieces of specialized equipment, with a specialized character, in the middle of a fantasy role-playing game. Your brain just has too many things that it can focus on. The pacing of a game can suddenly demand one's attention, convincing the emotional limbic system that some goals must be perceived as an emergency. Even once the pacing slows, other players could be distracted for the better part of an hour with a thousand tiny cognitive tasks — like organizing their equipment in a role-playing game.

Real Illusion

Just as easily as they snatch our attention away, the sense of space in video games can bring us closer to the things that really matter.

"He's in a horrible relationship and I am in a bad marriage," Shawnda says, but "after meeting face to face for the first time, we simply knew it was destiny."

American Shawnda Blansjaar first met another player, "Uzma," in the game Ryzom. Her story is punctuated by the good and bad both in and out of games. It was amidst guilds and groups breaking apart, moving between games, and settling in for good old in-game killing that she and her husband-to-be, a man from the Netherlands, began pouring their hearts out to one another. Before long it was clear he'd be needing to book a plane flight to the States.

Shawnda remembers the first visit. "I introduced him to Slurpees," she says, "He almost died of heat stroke in the desert's 115-degree heat!"

After marrying in 2006 and spending a month getting to know each other as husband and wife, Shawnda remembers thinking, "Obviously, one of us has to move." These days Shawnda and her daughter are loving everything about Holland, from the landscapes and language to the bicycles and the food. "Finally getting to be together and live together was a huge relief."

Though she says that there's "no substitute for actually being able to see him," she's still impressed by the ability that the game world had to bring a feeling of togetherness. "It's odd how 'playing' together in a game can make you forget that you're 6000 miles away."

There's an immersive quality that you really only get once a game gives you something, or someone, to fall in love with. Alternatively, finding something in games worth screaming about pulls you into other elements. In secondary worlds, some people embrace the dark and angry elements of their personalities, while others relish their ability to treat others fairly, give charitably, and love. And this all happens between real, living human beings. Your actions in secondary worlds affect flesh-and-blood people who also fundamentally reside in the primary, real world. Even if you don't think that games are real in any other sense, in some online spaces we face off with *real* people, spend our *real* time and money, experiencing media that walks the line between reality and illusion.

This realistic immersion can make it very difficult to avoid getting pulled into the world, because in many ways it transforms these spaces into *a part of* the real world. These worlds don't just immerse you with images of bloodthirsty space dragons; they immerse other real, live humans that play with you. In so doing, in letting you share that illusion, they make it all the more difficult to disbelieve.

"It was much pleasanter at home," cried Alice. "When one wasn't always growing larger and smaller, and being ordered about by mice and rabbits!" Alice, in Lewis Carroll's well-known story *Alice in Wonderland*, chased the white rabbit into a very real-feeling illusion. Games mix a similar level of reality and illusion; that's part of their allure. The high point of any story is when you realize that you've lost yourself in it.

While plain old offline games might just pull you in with the immersions we've already talked about, games that take players online raise the bar. They add to all of this a level of realism that regular games can't; they put you into a world that is, for lack of better words, really real. It's a strange thing, but sharing this space with other real people takes it beyond just illusory. It really *can* be like walking into a 24-hour diner in the primary world. What happens to the mind when it gets ordered around by a boss and a wife in one world, and rabbits and trolls in another? What about when the boss is actually playing the rabbit and the spouse is playing the troll? Components of the primary and secondary worlds are being mixed, confusing the senses.

Consider the thoughts of Gregory Bateson, the older scholar whom we brought up earlier. He wrote, "A man experiences the full intensity of subjective terror when a spear is flung at him out of the 3D screen or when he falls headlong from some peak created in his own mind in the intensity of a nightmare. At the moment of terror there was no questioning of 'reality,' but still there was no spear in the movie house and no cliff in the bedroom."[35]

The spear is still illusion, but what happens when five other people saw the same illusion? It's a hard question to answer: when an illusion is shared, *is it* really still fake, a facade? If that spear hits you, and causes some headaches for a group of other gamers that you're with within the game, then are you still just playing a game?

The digital living room, simple secondary worlds that allow these kinds of social connections, they're a different technology than video games alone. Just as television presents a more advanced experience than literature, and video games extend television, games that go online are giving us something beyond normal gaming. Some still give us all the hooks and immersions of video games. All of them are creating a space worth screaming about. There are a few scholars out there who are trying to help us to get a grip on the fact that we've gone beyond play. They're pointing out that MMO games, especially the complex commercial secondary worlds, are starting to approach the look and feel of real life in powerful new ways.[36]

Because secondary worlds introduce to digital technology much of the fullness and complexity which allows the primary world to grow, it is becoming harder to draw lines between them. Secondary worlds are rife with unique art, architecture, biology, physics, geology, mythology, economies, social orders and political structures. These are giving players inside a tangible sense that what's happening is real. The richness of these worlds taps all of these forms of immersion. Anthropologist Thomas Malaby suggests that "games" are similar to reality in that they offer persistence, the idea that they're "always on," as well as contingency, or a sense of chance. When anything can happen and events last, Malaby says, games "approach the texture of everyday life." They work enough like real life that they might as well be. As happens in the real world, you might never know the outcome of your actions. The secondary world brings out the possibility of losing when losing matters.

We aren't just playing in online worlds like EverQuest or World of Warcraft because they're fun. Sometimes we're getting screamed at. Sometimes we're falling in love. Most times, they're just a new part of the primary world. Some of these worlds aren't attractive purely because they are fun. Game-like online worlds aren't just secondary worlds in the sense that Tolkien was talking about. They don't *just* take the imagination on a convincing and wild ride, then stop once we've reached the end of the story. The digital living room doesn't disappear once we leave. It stays turned on, as near to 24-7 as possible. Some of the secondary worlds out there are so large that two people can play in one secondary world for years without ever meeting. This experience is still just coming from dots on a screen, it's still an illusion, but these worlds are convincing. Whether it's chance, persistence or anything else, there's no denying that experiences in some games are taking on the characteristics of our experiences in the real world. These worlds have created a real illusion, a paradox. A chimera of sorts.

When you bring together real people in real places, what happens isn't just good or bad. Our real world is full of poverty, charity, terrorism and heroism. When human beings come together in video games, the same is true. There are extreme cases being made for the good in games. Burn victims, kids with learning disabilities, post-traumatic stress victims; they've all enjoyed great helping hands because of gaming technology. Researchers have used games to give them some of the most effective treatment and attention in decades.

Because games are made and played by real people, they aren't just used for good ends. Some gamers in Russia have beaten in-game rivals to death; its been reported that violent gang members in Korea, America, and China have shot real live people who were their opponents inside the game world. Media experience, like everything else in life, is an experience. Having an experience while sitting behind a computer monitor doesn't make it less real; it doesn't magically take away the sting of being insulted, harassed or threatened by a real person. Sharing experiences with others can motivate people to great deeds, or it can drive foul and reprehensible acts. Once we take games online, what happens isn't going to be simply good or bad. It's going to be *human*.

While all games are necessarily real, in that playing them affects a person, MMO games and persistent worlds represent a higher level of realistic immersion. Secondary world takes on a new level of meaning. These "players" are in a digital living room that can stretch around the world. Creating and sharing experiences necessarily makes the game worlds as organic, authentic, genuine and real as the people populating them. Inside these worlds are real people, interacting with each other on their own terms. When somebody calls the experience "virtual" or "synthetic," they're incorrect in two ways. First, like with offline games, playing a game still affects our real-world bodies. Watching a television show always has some kind of affect, even if it was only to make us chuckle a couple of times. The chuckle chemicals in the brain were real, the sitting was relaxing, and so forth. Secondly, we don't say that telephone conversations are virtual, or fake, simply because a technology is working as a go-between for the two people who are talking. When two gamers interact in a secondary world, the game has connected them equally as much as a telephone has connected the two people having a phone conversation. The nature of the experience could be quite different, though in most games online their presence is felt.

Many of the people who play games like World of Warcraft are actually talking to other players with their real-world voices, just like they would do over the telephone. Depending on the world they're in they might see, hear, even attack and kill one another's characters. Secondary worlds are spaces that we walk around in, only it's an avatar, our graphical depiction, our puppet within the world. This puppet in the secondary world is doing the walking, talking, shooting, and/or flying. We're really only the puppeteers, controlling the action with a mouse, keyboard or other input device. These worlds are a step beyond simply being able to interact with a story, playing only with ourselves.

And we haven't exactly had a lot of time to understand them. At no other time in human history have twenty million people been able to meet and greet each other from their bedrooms, living rooms or offices — coming together in the same, shared, alternate reality. These "games" can pull us into secondary worlds with more force and skill than any other media before them. These are a media that give experiences to our real eyes, ears, hearts and brains; experiences that professionals painstakingly design to be fun, breathtaking, and exhilarating. We are put in control; it is our experience and we share it with others. This can blot out the rest of the world.

And every now and again, that can be wonderful. Can you imagine a world without music, theatre, or the basic elements of civilized society? Maybe for contemporary society it's television, MP3 players, and the internet, but without these things civilization as we know it wouldn't exist. Some media pass along our ideas, including our ideas on what it means to be human, and they can all make life a lot more colorful. Literature, film, even video games fit together in our long tradition of storytelling, our tradition of sharing experiences. They aren't going away.

According to Tolkien, all humans have an inborn need to experience all that they can and to "hold communion with other living things." Secondary worlds give us that, whether or not they're detailed and online. Today's most sophisticated games take us beyond ourselves in a way that just wasn't possible 20 or 30 years ago. Even if it's just for an instant, getting immersed into a new kind of place can grant an indescribable freedom. Some experiences refuel the soul. Stories bring perspective, refresh our minds, and can show us ways we might improve our reality with certain parts of the fantasy. We might not have seen those options if it weren't for the story.

The other side of this coin is that stories can overstep their boundaries, when not many people understand how to protect themselves from that. A secondary world that blots out or takes over your world isn't making your life better. It's replacing your life. Sometimes only a fine line separates fun from this kind of escapism. If a good game can pull us in, does a responsible game then help us to get back out again?

A major part of the challenge being called "game addiction" has nothing to do with addiction. It has to do with the fact that our puny human brains have a difficult time being in two places at once. Going between these primary and the secondary realities can be perplexing. Even before we talk about addiction, whether in neurochemistry, psychology, or any other area, we've got to acknowledge that the gaming experience alone can exert a forceful pull, even with the simple tradition of immersion.

More than anything, secondary worlds challenge us. On the one hand, they aren't just letting gamers play as heroes and villains. Games are capable of connecting the world's living rooms. We can taste the glory of being a hero, the pain of the villain, all in worlds that lack the finality of reality. Sometimes it's this experience of playing the hero that gives a gamer far more inspiration than any piece of literature or film could ever hope to deliver.

Though immersion into a game is a prerequisite to addiction, the opposite isn't always true. Even though video games are only a few decades old, they've already woven themselves deeply into our reality. Right this second, people are playing online with good friends and lovers. Sometimes they also play with people who make their lives more difficult. Gamers play with people from all around the world, and the choices that they are making right now could have major implications for the technologies *everybody* will be seeing in just five or ten years. Video games are just pictures on a screen, but they have far-reaching effects which most people just don't grasp yet. Games are compelling. A lot of that comes down to how our physical bodies make sense of the illusions that they see on the screen. They seem real. Sometimes, they actually are.

Three

WHY THEY PLAY

A boat can float in water, but it can sink in it also. — Chinese proverb, also from *Legend of the Drunken Master*

Games are carefully crafted to be exciting, satisfying and rewarding; the word that some like to throw around is *fun*. Once immersion takes hold, a player's experience of a game becomes far more natural. They aren't slapping on a keyboard so much as looking into the secondary world for an experience. They act and react. Much of what keeps them inside only happens on the inside, once immersion into the experience is more automatic than not. Today, when that same immersion is directed at older media, the conclusion of addiction isn't normally jumped to; books, movies and plays are more seen as a part of human life worth keeping.

It's been some time since burning the books, crushing the film canisters and executing the playwrights was a big priority for society in general. Though games seem the vogue moral panic, when a full-fledged experience is available at a gamer's beck and call, they sometimes aren't seeking entertainment so much as another place, another part of their lives. To understand why somebody would abandon reality and give preference to that place, we have to understand what that place offers above and beyond reality. It can be a confusing prospect when a space that we enter, a place for experiencing, is bandied about as entertainment. A family might travel to a theme park, but it's rare to find one who spends six hours of every day inside. Oftentimes the people, places, sights and sounds in secondary worlds invite us to forge real, meaningful relations with other living people, sometimes with the history and complexity of a world. Forces we find in everyday experience can keep a person from moving away from a game world that's gotten out of hand. Many of the approaches towards understanding a gamer's drive to play tell us why a gamer supposes they play a game, but not how those motivations might be in any way different from what motivates a person to visit any other part of their world.

Is it possible that, at least in some ways, gamers are having more than everyday experience? Not only do games trick our senses and immerse us with their texture, experiences inside good games are presumably designed to be better on some level or another. We enter that other place of entertainment, the theme park, because a roller coaster gives us something not normally available during the daily grind. The in-game play, the in-game shopping, the in-game sex, if it can be put together in a way that's somehow more pleasing, we might assume that designers will try to meet that mark.

If even the physical experience of play can hold human attention for too long, then what kind of power would a world hold if the events which transpired inside were always more exciting or meaningful? Most gamers don't have the first clue about how their bodies take in a game; how games immerse them in the experience. With physical immersion already acting as a kind of glue, a gamer's own tangible likes and dislikes in gaming, like plot, characters, and gameplay, can bring about an invisible undertow. Though most players have an easy time pinning down things in a game that excite them, the most powerful motivators often sit just outside conscious perception. Even the most seasoned among the ranks of gamers might be caught unawares. In an odd way, one such situation seemed to explode for longtime gamer and blogger Dave Yeager.

You Can Always Get What You Want

"I used to joke that I was Jack Thompson for a day," he muses. For Dave to be compared to Mr. Thomson, the outspoken paragon of ignorant and misdirected views on gaming, is a badge of honor for those with a sense of irony. Before tens of thousands of angry gamers stormed Dave's blog, *Soul Kerfuffle*, he recalls his thoughts on addiction before any of the madness. "As a gaming geek, I was firmly on the side of gaming addiction being total nonsense. Somewhere between skeptical and dismissive." At the same time, he hadn't seen his friend Andy in awhile.

"Andy was becoming kind of a mess; I mean, he was playing and working on the game constantly. After I quit the game, a good while before he did, I basically didn't see or hear from him for months. Nobody else really did either, at least not out and about in the 'real world,' as it were. Then, one day, he just told me, 'I've got to quit this game.'"

Dave suggested that Andy write down some of his thoughts for their close friends on Dave's blog. In the blink of an eye, *Soul Kerfuffle* went from getting one or two visits a day to getting tens of thousands. Over two years later Dave still receives stories from gamers who, as he puts it, "don't know where else to turn." In the midst of the early madness, however, many of the emails were not friendly.

When asked to rate the initial viciousness, he said, "If 1 is 'you're a jerk' and 10 is 'I'll kill you if I see you,' definitely a 10. It made me kind of sad, because this is the kind of thing that makes people dismissive of gamers in general."

When Dave followed up with one of the most incensed of the gamers, he was confronted with a puzzling notion. He explains, "The reason at least some of these hardcore folks get upset was not because of the marginalization of their hobby. People who quit the game are seen in extremely harsh terms by the hardest of the hard core," Dave says. "The major problem these guys had with Andy's post didn't have anything to do with Warcraft. It had to do with *quitting* Warcraft."

Quit Warcraft, and suddenly you've created more work for these other players. Dave goes on, saying that these players wanted Andy to "find a balance somewhere." "Now their notion of 'balance,' mind you, was playing a lot more than I ever played even in my most intense period. Even though there was a grain of salt to be taken there, the notion was interesting."

The reasons that drive gamers to play, or to stop playing, have perplexed and excited researchers since the 1970s, the time of word-based MUD worlds. Game designers and researchers alike have approached the topic of gamer motivation. Dozens of journal articles, news pieces and books go into what drives gamers. Sony Online Entertainment even opened up their MMO game Everquest II, providing terrabytes of information to well-known researchers.[1] Past video game-related work has looked at how learning can inspire play, the influence of deep, inner feelings and how certain players gravitate towards certain archetypes once they start gaming.[2]

Some people like to say that there's nothing new under the sun. Others have said that while this view very often has merit, some of what's happening in the digital landscape *is* new.[3] Though many of the symbols, archetypes and stories in games are things that we've seen before, even simple things like walking around inside a secondary world require learning. Using the example of chess, even going from one game to another sometimes means learning about new kinds of "moves," "strategies," even unique opponents. In any new game, one must often master the new concepts in order to win. In today's video games, making that fun is the rough job of the game designer. Longtime gamers, in many ways, aren't all that different from the Compagnons, the journeymen of medieval and modern-day France. Whatever their trade, journeyman go between a number of different shops on a Tour de France, working to perfect their trade. Games are new enough that going into them isn't always easy, not yet anyway, and a serious part of the game's enjoyment comes from a kind of journeyman effect, the sustained positive feedback, or pleasure, of learning in continuously morphing venues.

"Fun," the elusive beast that designers angle for, might be just the joy that we get from learning how a new game works. That's one of the major ideas the book *A Theory of Fun for Game Design*, by game designer Raph Koster, mentioned earlier.[4] This was a book researched and imagined by the same man who researched and imagined many parts of the game Star Wars Galaxies, a commercial secondary world which kept me playing in ways that will be mentioned later. Suffice it to say, it's safe to assume that Raph knows a thing or two about fun. He settles on the idea that fun truly is about learning. When we play a game, what we're really doing is figuring out (he calls it "grokking") a new system, a new kind of experience. It's that feeling of understanding, and eventually mastery, which makes us feel good about playing. A lot of his book works as an explanation as to why the inherent human need to feel accomplished is something that games are apt to satisfy.

The joy of learning, however, doesn't usually go on forever. Koster notes that once a player groks a game, once they've learned as much as they care to, it loses a lot of its flair. After they understand the best path from point A to point B, there are only so many times that some paths can be traveled before they become passé. The natural course is to put the game down. Like the journeymen, they move to the next game. The next lesson.

Is staying on the move the key to enjoying games more generally? With all of the different games out there, players can take what they've learned in one game, put it to use in the next, and enjoy the thrill of putting those puzzle pieces together. There's a satisfaction in entering games, learning how they work, and understanding what it is that you've learned.

But this game learning isn't the same thing as picking up French, Russian, or particle physics. Well-designed games don't pull people in with book learning; instead, what they're doing is making it fun and exciting to learn the adventure of your choice.

This is easy learning, idealized learning, usually with happy endings. In seeking fun, we pick up skills *incidentally*. We may learn to navigate a new type of interface, learn tidbits about ancient Chinese art, but more for the pleasure than to obtain skills. The problem here is that by creating easily learned and ultra-satisfying realities, we may be creating bad standards for when our actual bodies need to learn primary world lessons. If we get used to real-feeling worlds which are ever easy to master and satisfying to be in, worlds where we get to choose when and where we get what we want, then does this make painstaking and difficult real-world learning even *less* attractive? If it's a choice between learning that Russian, or learning one more of the many fun games that we have the option to enter, how likely is it that we're going to pick the Russian?

Then again, maybe games haven't taught Russian and Spanish to the gamers of the world because nobody has taken the time to transform "Ultimate Parruski Challenge" and "Extreme Espanol Escapades" into blockbuster-quality video games. Then again, maybe gamers from around the world are learning English because it has become the lingua franca among European gamers choosing to enter secondary worlds. If learning Russian and Spanish were each incidental skills that had to be picked up in order to play inside the most attractive and well designed games, perhaps the gamers of the world would have picked them up already.

Where many influential scholars take the position that video games foster new and important kinds of learning, learning that education systems could be wholly ignoring, many developmental psychologists are highly skeptical.[5] Though this is a topic more fully covered in Chapter Five, *Games Are Not Babysitters*, some scholars worry that the new kinds of communication, with emphasis on text and a lack of physical presence, the googling, the texting, are adding to the difficulty for young people to grow skills in traditional ways of obtaining knowledge and relating to people.[6] While there are certainly many new types of knowledge, from relational to information processing, that are becoming important if not vital, it will be some time before a concrete middle ground is reached.

In the midst of the concerns and the enthusiasm, some scholars are looking for a resurgence of traditionally shunned games, like poker. "...Online poker lets the world play. Poker could offer a far more friendly and engaging American face to the globe in cyberspace," says professor Charles Nesson of Harvard University.

Professors like Nesson are proposing that we take a second look at these traditional games, most visibly poker. His Global Poker Strategic Thinking Society, besides having a comically large name, is seeking to further a global poker society that encourages learning throughout the world. On its website, Nesson discusses the skills taught by the game. "First is the skill of recognizing and making good investments of your resources while avoiding making bad ones. Second is the skill of reading your opponent's strategy without revealing your own. These are useful skills for moving successfully not only at a poker table but as well in law, business and romance."[7] Whatever we can say about its applicability, learning as a key motivator for gaming is one of the more popular notions out there.

A few scholars recently made headlines when they connected a lesser-known Freudian notion to games. They said that we don't go into games simply because there are dragons to be slain, or pirates to be hunted — instead they suggested that we go in because games let us satisfy certain deep-seated psychological needs.[8] Universal needs, like feeling accomplished, in control and connected with others. The assumption is that while they might obtainable, elsewhere in the primary world, they aren't always easy to find. It's not always easy to jump from one to another. Where addictive games could keep us coming back, even if we're not enjoying ourselves, a game that can fulfill these core needs might bring our real-world selves satisfaction that we might not find anywhere else. This notion was even developed into a business, where scholars look to show game developers how to design these needs satisfactions into their game, ostensibly just to improve the fun factor.[9]

In Maslow's pyramid of needs, after all, it's the self-actualizing goals, what we seek out once we've got food and shelter, which tend to give us the most powerful satisfaction. Besides the three above, Maslow might suppose that humans have lofty needs to chase knowledge and seek beauty. Maybe these games can give us some of the bigger and badder thrills in life, and in so doing increase our well-being in both the primary and the secondary worlds.

Whether it's dragons or pirates, goals or needs, play has to be driven by something. Though designing the rewarding behavior into games often means setting up goals that players don't notice, it's the icing over the cake, how the game looks, that actually helps it speak to a player. Without that, well designed goals and game design are meaningless.[10] Game designer Steve Swink uses the example of a car racing game, showing that even small changes to a game's icing can fundamentally change what we get from it. In his example, we've swapped our Porsche and our Lamborghini for something ... else. He writes, "...Substitute for the car a giant, balding fat guy running as fast as he possibly can spraying sweat like a sprinkler in August. Without altering the structure of the game, the tuning of the game, or the function of the game, the feel of the game is substantially altered."[11]

Raph Koster uses the example of a chess set. As a game, chess is really only about the moves that are available to you. You can move your king in a certain way, a pawn in another, and your rooks and bishops in others. If you take away the titles of the pieces, however, the game suddenly becomes a lot less regal. Attaching powerful-sounding names makes the pieces symbolic.[12] The game can represent more to the people playing. Chess probably wouldn't have had lasted nearly so long if it were just about moving around nondescript pieces of tree bark. Even checkers, points out Koster, uses the symbolic language of "king me" in order to make it a little bit more courtly.

Richard Bartle co-created the first of the MUDs, the secondary worlds built entirely from text. He was one of the first to work at identifying the different ways to play in these worlds and is credited for the notion that different types of players may have been going in to be one of our four major player types in wordy worlds: the socializers, explorers, achievers, and killers.[13] The names pretty much say it all; Bartle's suggestion is that certain people like doing certain things, and a game ecosystem can only support so many of each type. More recently, a few scholars have put numbers to these player motivations, showing that it's possible to separate players in such a way. Among other things, from these studies we know players likely also go in for escapism and role-play.[14]

One of the first steps to understanding addiction is knowing someone's reasoning behind picking up a controller, turning on a computer or flipping open their Nintendo DS. As a starting point for today's games, it works well to break players into groups of socializers, achievers, explorers, escapists, and so forth. Few if any players might fit exclusively into any one of these groups, but that's good. The point of the groupings is to help us get a very basic handle on what players are doing in today's worlds. When we step back, however, we see that most of these groupings are ultimately organized into two major reasons to play: the *people* and the *game*. Note that these trace back directly to the two secret ingredients: social connectivity and game design. My early thesis research found this distinction to be the only one to separate, under stringent regression analysis, "addicts" from those whose high levels of play may not have been unhealthy.[15] This was under a fairly stringent scale for "addiction," one which separated it from players whose high amounts of play may not have carried as many ill effects. Though my research had major limitations, it's an interesting notion.[16]

It bears mentioning that every person inside a secondary world is an individual. Like anyone else, a gamer's experience of playing, how they see things inside a secondary world, will be shaped by their brains, bodies, and experiences in and out of games. Different players in the same game will see the same things a little different. Commonalities and variations between *games* are just as important to understanding why players play in certain ways. As game designers dictate the experience, it's possible that archetypes may change with the types of games available. Fishermen use different kinds of bait to catch different kinds of fish. Most of the secondary worlds out right now, whether they're a single-player game, a virtual world like Second Life, or a major commercial MMO game like

World of Warcraft, drop different lures. You could call these differences, like a game's use of humor, the specific types of combat it offers, even the branding of the company it comes from, structural characteristics. They're the varied structures that gamers acknowledge, disdain, and/or latch onto when they play the game.[17] And in early research, players who self-reported having more potent problems playing did seem to prefer certain structural characteristics beyond just preference for the people and game, in lower-order forms of data analysis such as correlations.[18]

Even though researchers have made great contributions in the areas of motivations, player types, and a game's structures, they have traditionally been limited by the fact that they can only ask for participation. As more game developers open up their doors to researchers, however, providing exact data on demographics, researchers will have more and more exact data on how players use things like structural characteristics, the parts of the game that are designed. Those are going to be a lot of fun for running statistics, longitudinal analysis, and all other manner of high nerdery, because having that data tells us exactly what the player is doing.

At the same time, obtaining data from gamers themselves might possibly be a different story. Even when someone means to respond to a questionnaire truthfully (an issue brought up among academics even with excellent types of data), they don't always assess themselves correctly.[19] This has been a longstanding problem for research surveys; the problem is compounded in self-administration of surveys over the internet. When people take surveys themselves, there are a number of reasons they commonly under- or over-report different factors. Respondents might not understand a question's meaning correctly, especially if it's about a complicated concept in psychology. If you're asking a question about body weight, especially if you're asking it of a gamer who is looking to wrap up the questionnaire quickly, they may answer approximately, rather than take the time to weigh themselves. They may not even have a scale. Some people have gone so far as to suggest that tiny changes in wording, especially in psychological surveys, can fundamentally change their meaning.[20]

Our understanding of what motivates players is growing, and games research is slowly leaving its adolescence. The research has progressed quickly and cleanly. It has not fully matured because the games have not fully matured. We can talk about "killers," or how causing grief for fellow players satisfies certain intrinsic needs, or even how vicious attitudes among specific gamers correlate to certain structural characteristics within a game. We could run numbers through a supercomputer, calculate the variables, make sure that the "killers" won't ruin our brand new game for the "escapists," "socializers," or anyone else. But what if it's a romance game that we're making? The games industry is built from innovation; ultimately it has only begun to explore the possibilities of how it designs the real illusion. The "killers" might tell themselves that all's fair in love and war, though maybe those poor, misunderstood "killers" are just looking for love; could the romance game, how it's designed and deployed, soothe the troubled soul of a particular killer?

We don't know how effective these models are even now, because players aren't forced to choose the same personality twice in online games. Presumably they'll find new satisfactions, whether to their self-actualizing needs or their most dark and dank desires, in new games. The research so far does highlight one very clear motivation to play: easy agency, or our ability to cherry-pick the experiences that we want. We can be the killers one minute, and the next we're a balding, sweaty, fat man who can run hundreds of miles per hour. No two people's wants or needs are exactly the same, and sometimes what we want changes daily. We may have certain basic needs, but there isn't one single thing which satisfies those for everyone. Humans aren't simple.

We've all got different ideas on what kind of icing we want in our cakes, in our worlds. Whether in real life or in our game lives, we all have different hobbies and desires. Some people want to be heroic wizards, but others want to be romantic Italians, dramatic high-schoolers, or rustic fishermen. Whether in a game or in real life, it's always nice to see those fantasies come true. And oftentimes people pick fantasies that they can fulfill in reality. Let's say that a man's deep inner desire is to travel. In real life, he can do just that. He can save up a little bit of money, buy his choice of luggage, and then go on his trip — whether it's backpacking in the South Island of New Zealand, taking a luxurious Caribbean cruise, or finally visiting his extended family in rural China. He has the ability to choose.

Really loving a game doesn't come explicitly from just a satisfying design, or just the icing that you see. On one level there's a gestalt that we'll get to in the next chapter; on another level there's a fun freedom to having places that take all of the troubles and worries out of our choices. In games, not only can you ride on horseback through rugged terrain, but there's no thousand-dollar plane ticket, no excessive fees for renting the horse, and you can ride the terrain with people from all over the globe. It's easy. The agency becomes more automatic, more fluid. You aren't over-burdened with the financial ramifications of getting an iPhone or a plane ticket. You click a few buttons.

In games, desires become whims; we can become comic book heroes, create dragon-riding barbarians, or manufacture a devastating fleet of spaceships. Or we can take our pick, depending on how we're feeling on a particular day. We have a level of agency that's beyond even the rising tide of technological agency out and about in the real world.

The themes in most of the games out there are easy to consume, but also easy to grasp. Many non-gamers have this perception that these spaces are foreign, nerdy and unforgiving. Though in some ways that's the case, where it takes time for the brain and body to learn what it needs for full immersion, a game's themes are often pretty straightforward. There may be dragons, space travel or other fantasy objects, but in an age of hobbits and *Star Wars*, fantasy is a notion that most people can understand. Most games replicate a lot of what we expect to see in real life. Things like drag-ons and aliens and pirates may not be too prevalent in our realities, but they're things that we see on billboards, read in stories, and hear about on the radio. We know what they are.

Gamers present and future will walk away from a game having actu-ally participated in an unreal or amazing story. Games do go beyond sto-ries, even television shows; a player hasn't just read about high adventure, striving in the face of ambiguous morality, or any other hero's challenge. Perhaps more important is that a player is constantly able to pick and choose between many such experiences. People who step back into the world having done that are faced with a double-edged sword; the rewards may not carry over into everyone else's reality—but that person's mind has still walked some impressive road.

Regardless of what the future holds, even today we have more sophis-ticated games, and more of them, than ever before; if you know how to play one, then chances are you'll be able to learn the basics of many more.

It's part of what makes them fun, after all. You can pretty much pick the game, or the experience, that you want. Today's entertainment offers a powerful new form of agency, more choices than we sometimes know what to do with, combined with a fluid ease with which we can pluck those ripe choices from their respective homes. Even a basic knowledge of today's entertainment lets someone choose between the music, television program, or game that best suits them. Whether or not regular people are aware of it, they understand how to navigate between a dizzying and growing number of venues for experiencing their world, a freedom that few other humans besides royalty and the rich have had before.

With television we "channel surf" until we find the show we want to watch. With the World Wide Web, we "web surf" until we find the web page that's got what we want. With video games we surf between the games, and within the games, until we find the activity that suits us. Our entire world is made to satisfy us with media experience: stories and experiences that, more often than not, are inconvenient or impossible for us to have ourselves. And nowhere is this agency or ease more the rule than within a video game. A contemporary MMO game offers more than any other single game could.

Players in the massive, online secondary worlds have an infinite number of little activities that they can surf between. There are more ways to play, more things to see, and more fights to be won than could be done in a lifetime. Not only do players usually run one or two programs *while* playing the game, they can kill drakes, fly over skyscrapers, and work with other living players in ways that will make even a repetitive media experience a little bit different every time.

Sometimes the side-along programs are made to let players get more out of their games; some of them are even being created for use in just one or two specific games. Voice chat programs have been created specifically for use in video games, such as, Ventrilo or Teamspeak. Certain websites have been created to provide information on specific MMO games. The websites thottbot.com, wowwiki.com and wowhead.com all serve the game World of Warcraft. Skilled players will get specific types of information from all three, depending on what they need. Sometimes the programs being used might or might not have anything to do with the game. These might include free instant message programs like internet relay chat (IRC), AOL instant messenger (AIM), guild forums, community websites or email.

The level of agency invading our lives rises above what's been at most of humankind's fingertips in the past few thousand years. While people around the world are learning to deal with on-demand cable, tiny phones that go anywhere, and wealth that spews from tiny plastic cards, gamers have more options and more agency than those accustomed only to other cutting-edge technologies. In just a single game they have the agency to watch, connect, spend, and, in a heady philosophic sense, live. Immersion, when poorly understood, can keep our physical bodies transfixed, whether by sights which carry the texture of reality, a multitude of events to which we pay our attention, or the artistry and the presence of living human beings, in all of their baffling and lovable complexity.

But it's the events which occur during that time when immersion has taken hold that take us beyond any experience now available in reality. A critical aspect to understanding gaming addiction is to break down exactly how media experiences are heightened. In many cases the texture of gaming environments convince our minds and bodies that what we're seeing in the secondary world is a tactile reality, but in other ways these worlds have been designed to go beyond what's possible in the primary world. All the journeyman gamer need do to find it is to keep journeying.

A State of Becoming

At my worst, I was playing twenty, perhaps twenty-two hours every day. I had just finished my undergraduate program at the University of Washington, had just broken up with a girlfriend of three years, and was applying for jobs. As the weeks went by, there were no hires. No interviews. No more applications. No new games. There was only Sony's Star Wars Galaxies, first designed to encourage complex socialization, a vicious commercial marketplace, and intense combat. For me, playing it meant mastering a dozen professions, exploring hundreds of cities, and making tens of millions of credits, the in-game currency. The next thing I knew was the amazing relief of being on a plane to New Zealand. Shaking my head, one thought would not stop recurring.

"I wonder if I'm ever going to touch that game again."

The answered came almost as a reflex.

"Probably."

A lot happened in the next few months. In between remote hikes on the South Island of New Zealand, an email let me know that I'd been accepted to graduate school. After precious few other events, I was staring into that game again, taking cantina dancers on intergalactic shopping sprees, outdoing all but a handful of other merchant-barons, and battling Jedi with my regular, non–Jedi character.

For twelve hours at a time I wasn't consciously aware of the part of me drinking coffee by the pint, eating little, and losing weight at a steep pace. The pull to play almost seemed to come from outside myself; my eyes in no way transfixed on a simple computer monitor. Rather my attention went between collecting lightsaber crystals, obtaining art and artifacts for my business, and sauntering from battle to battle, never really taking time away from mortal danger.

And then my attention was focused on the 23-inch, fifty-pound computer monitor which sat on a hardwood floor, surrounded by detritus. It was the first and last time in my life I would ever really get high. I had smoked more marijuana that night than at any time in my life. Only in the one altered state did I fully recognize the other. Less than a week after, I flew to Hawaii and to graduate school. Without a computer.

All games are, more or less, human: another place to experience something. You can get the exciting, fluffy, and triumphant emotions. You can also get the spiteful, dramatic, and vengeful, especially where other living people are involved. Even though you can't smell, touch, or smile in the presence of the game's programmed characters, or even another real person in the world, what's striking is the power of the emotions you can have regardless. The presence of other people in the game does, without a doubt, make everything inside a secondary world more pertinent.

How, then, do we begin to explain the strength of a game's initial pull? Immersion only greases the wheels. Its effect on a person's senses does keep us playing, can provide subtle pulls and state changes which appeal to some, but immersion tends not to provide the tangible draws. Things like structural characteristics, player motivations, or other psychological concepts found in reality *start* to explain what we're looking for. These all give us insight into why the player *thinks* he or she is playing, reasons rooted in primary-world motivations that sometimes even dictate where in the game a player spends his time, but they don't provide the whole story. Gaming provides new motivations, the likes of which have few counterparts in the psychology of traditional experience.

As "real illusions," these gaming experiences are a chimera. They are the mixture of an experience that looks and feels like reality, yet is designed to present to the player the sensation that they are more. To get some perspective on why this is so powerful, it's necessary to step inside the way-back machine.

In the 1600s, French philosopher René Descartes noted that the human body wasn't always quite so powerful in its abilities as the mind could be in its ambitions. He distinguished between the human body, which he saw as an imperfect machine in many ways and, the perfect soul.[21] When a gamer peers into the worlds inside his computer, the characters he's put in control of are, in ways, "more perfect." The gamer is afforded new kinds of skills and abilities, the likes of which can empower a gamer on levels that may flit just beneath their conscious awareness. Cheating death, jumping great distances, going warp speed, we could fill this entire book with examples of gaming abilities not possible for your average contemporary human. As repetitive as the book might get, should it be filled with such examples, it would only scratch the surface.

It's not just that in games we can select the experience we most want; games don't *just* provide agency or the appropriation of gaming skills. Some of a game's pull comes from the nature of the heightened experience. Games provide what might be best called a Cartesian chimera. On the one hand, the texture of a good gaming experience, the persistence and contingency discussed heretofore, works with a gamer's relative skill at immersion to keep his mind and body from realizing that what he's seeing is illusory on some level.[22] On many levels, it's no illusion. This texture allows an actual form of empowered being. Simply being exposed to "more perfect" versions of ourselves, the pure experience of imaginative immersions, can be deeply fulfilling. Our minds are set free to explore and exercise heightened abilities and senses in a space that still looks and feels real. What happens inside seems like any other experience in life, yet provides more intense ability.

As it happens, in the last few years we've observed some interesting things about the brain's ability to pick up these new senses. Some technologies help blind people to see using only pinpricks on their tongues. Some similar technologies have displayed visual images by placing pads on a person's back. Some senses have even been created — those which no human has been known to have. When technology creates ways for us to see or experience something new, how often do we want to give that up? Craving access to technology like the internet, telephones, even games, might be tied to the brain's desire to keep in contact with the senses we learn.

From studying people who've lost limbs, we know that their minds have the capacity to "feel" their presence. We call this phantom limb pain. Many people desperately want these pieces of themselves back, even long after they're gone. By wearing a buzzing belt, a British man's sense of touch allowed him to automatically detect magnetic north. There's space in our brains for many different kinds of senses, often all that we really lack is the physical hardware. But what happens when that hardware is taken away? "For six weird weeks in the fall of 2004, Udo Wächter had an unerring sense of direction.... [He wore] a wide beige belt lined with 13 vibrating pads — the same weight-and-gear modules that make a cell phone judder. On the outside of the belt were a power supply and a sensor that detected Earth's magnetic field. Whichever buzzer was pointing north would go off. Constantly."[23]

The man wearing the compass belt truly loved it. He felt more confident, began realizing new ways that he could improve his life, even had dreams that incorporated the buzzing. The attachment caused his mind to rewire other senses, like touch, so that they could incorporate this new direction-sense. After the experiment ended and he relinquished the device, he was enormously upset, frequently getting lost in cities, even reporting "phantom buzzing" on a par with the phantom limb pain experienced by amputees. Other users who lost use of the belt reported feeling dizzy, disoriented, and a sensation that the world had become less predictable.

Was removing the belt tantamount to taking away a newly grown limb? More importantly, what does the mind lose when such a limb is taken away? What kinds of effects could that have on human psychology as we know it?

Games are rewiring the brain, teaching it new ways of being. What makes these motivations powerful, sometimes on levels that those using the technology don't even recognize, are the ways that they extend possibilities, sometimes beyond what users would expect even from other secondary worlds. Many games feature a built-in compass and map feature. In the game Alien vs. Predator, different types of players, for instance aliens and humans, are each allowed at least a couple of different ways that they can visually perceive the game world, like infrared vision, pheromone sensation, or night vision. While most games have map and compass features, sensations are only one small aspect of how they take on and extend the possibilities of human experience. These heightened perceptions and abilities are more than just satisfying your everyday deep-seated needs, or even elements of your personality type. Players can go after real-feeling experiences of objectives and fantasies never before physically present in reality. They provide the experience that we are more perfect.

Games take our senses beyond the confines of reality *and* they expand our expectations beyond what's available in life. Part of our desire to play comes from using computers as a type of a limb: monitors as a kind of "eye," headphones as "ears," a keyboard, mouse or input device as "motor skills," allowing us to move about. At the same time, those sensations also allow the inflation and extension of our *consciousness*. This does not happen in a spiritual sense that science cannot quantify, like perhaps a person's claims of astral projection or out-of-body experiences. The experiences being enabled by this limb are being measured daily. You can't tame a dragon in reality. You can't conquer a galaxy. Removing this limb hurts.

In the game Dungeon Keeper, what's called a "God game," players can do all sorts of unsavory, super-powered things. They can physically pick up monsters and drop them on heroes, or into a gladiator pit. In the Civilization games, players can research the atom, build nukes, and nuke enemy cities. In many different games, you can enter George Lucas's *Star Wars* universe, master the lightsaber, use the force, and wreak havoc on galaxies.

New technology isn't just about new senses — the limbs, but unique ways of being — what the limb provides. When a gamer stops entering secondary worlds, or even a single world, the need to re-enter a game may have everything to do with losing a real part of themselves. Whether the pull that they feel is gentle or overpowering, in many ways it's nothing new. Think about the last time that you couldn't find a particular picture or photo album. Maybe Aunt Maggie wanted to see, "that really hot guy from that club in Singapore," or maybe you just wanted the nostalgia of seeing someone from deep in your past. Maybe you and a friend had an argument about a detail in the picture, like whether the World Trade Center was in the backdrop when you visited New York City. In each case, the photos are a very real kind of a limb, an extension of your ability to see into the past, or across space. Like some other media experiences, photographs extend your eyes beyond their usual confines.[24] Though you can't physically interact with most photographs on the level you can a game world, for instance tilting the camera angle to the left, or physically breaking objects inside, they still help us to share experience in a very specific, very useful way.

These technologies, like any other tool that we use on a day-to-day basis, extend natural human ability. The history of the world is reflected in this increasing power of media experience to pull the senses into the fiction and nonfiction of our world. Wrote Marshall McLuhan, in 1964, "In the electric age, when our central nervous system is technologically extended to involve in the whole of mankind and to incorporate the whole of mankind in us, we necessarily participate."[25] McLuhan saw pictures as though they were tools, just a hammer or a saw. A hammer extends our ability to pound nails. A saw extends our ability to cut lumber. The gamer may not have any good way to compensate for the tools' removal, since certain tools are required to build skyscrapers, boats, and homes. The phantom pain is partly due to the feeling of using a tool, perhaps needs being met or their psychology inside, though it's also about the types of things which cannot ever be done without that particular technology.

What the unique gamer has learned to do inside combines with what the unique game provides. Though video games may pull on traditional notions of human psychology, whether in motivation, personality or any other field, we must not forget that video games are also designed. There is an interplay between the characteristics of every unique person using this limb with the characteristics of every unique media experience entered.

Whatever the advantages of a game's design, there's one thing that a game's charms are likely never to replace: the company of people. Real, living and breathing humans. The game designers make it easy for us to connect with experiences. They even design those experiences to be intrinsically more perfect, pleasurable, and intense. And while, so far as we know, they can't convincingly create people, they can connect them. Part of the charm in a secondary world, or even a simple board game, comes from interactions with other people. What happens when you give two people their own superpowers and the agency to decide how they'll use them, and then put them in the same room? What happens when it's ten people? A hundred? A thousand?

The Tribe Has Spoken

After Andrew had written about his moment in front of the mirror and after Dave had posted the ordeal online, the level of anger expressed by gamers was staggering. Dave wanted to show another side to the issue, so he contacted Andrew's in-game friend Kateri. "When we made those posts, the reaction was kind of ridiculous," Kateri remembers. She was in the same position as Andrew; both were officers in a guild that had gone from being "social," focused on relationships and personality, to "raiding," focused on completing the different goals for a game. As their guild made that change, it was clear to her that some people took things too far. It was also unclear what, as a rule, was unhealthy.

"I was never able to figure out the line. You get out of it what you put into it, in a real sense. The time, the grind. I think people get caught up in needing to be the best." Sighing, she says, "It's a bad thing when it starts to become all that matters."

Andrew, on the other hand, was fairly certain that the focus on raiding was that line. He says, "It's very easy to cross, or at least it was for me. It happens when the game and the achievement of 'in game goals' becomes more important than the people trying to achieve them." What he saw that finally "put things into a damning perspective" was that for a full year, people had worked to create bonds, create friendships. And then, he says, "We just forgot about them."

Kateri also made it clear that becoming more goal-oriented brought on discouraging changes in their guild. "People start cutting throats and leaving their friends behind, don't help each other out and don't care about the other people. It's uncomfortable, but it's a personal thing of where your line is. Some people can go further with it than others." As for Kateri, she was able to earn a graduate degree while playing three to four nights a week, "at Harvard, no less."

Though some games can offer more than reality, games with people sweeten that pot. As agency gets easier, the selected experiences more potent, in certain ways being inside a game also adds ease and potency to sociability. But if living, breathing people are major players in making these games more attractive, isn't that contradictory to thinking of games as "addictive?" Out and about in the real world, most don't tend to see meaningful relationships with meaningful people as addictions. But then by certain accounts, there are times when the people inside games are seen more or less as simple objects, a means to a game's designed end. If that were the case, people's colorful personalities painted over by objectification, would we still be right to call these relationships meaningful? If gamers were starting to view each other as just another tool for having an experience, then who would be responsible? In reality, architecture and the design of a space is enough to influence how people behave.[26] Humans sit on certain benches before others, walk certain paths before others. In games, architecture can be molded without brick, steel, carpenters or heavy machinery. Players can be and are, in many games, rewarded for interacting with other players in very specific ways. These rewards can come into a game in a thousand different ways, some of which may well influence whether a player tends to objectify the people whom he meets inside the real illusion.

One way to design interaction is through player interdependencies.[27] In the original design of the MMO game Star Wars Galaxies, a single player could master only two or three professions. And mastery took time. Some professions were based around combat, some around locating raw materials, some around creating items with those materials, some around selling those items. There were architects, doctors, beastmasters, musicians, and dancers. Each of these professions had something to offer others. Doctors, dancers, and singers improved a player's health and spirits in ways that were normally necessary for basic combat. Genetic engineers could create the most ferocious and coveted of pets for the beastmasters. If a player were to die, he or she would need extensive work from less skilled doctors, who sometimes paid for the opportunity to heal wounds. It helped them to become more powerful more quickly.

Player interdependencies are just one slice of what's called social embedding, where player interrelations and interactions are expected to erupt and grow during the lifetime of a gamer's stay in any one game world. Looking at the end-result social game, when people start pouring in, you can separate social embedding into two major categories. The first is the mechanical, those places where the game developers have put careful thought into planning situations where players' paths will cross and continue to cross. While player interaction is often *extramechanical,* that is spontaneous, unplanned or unrewarded within the framework of the game's framework for distributing power, a great deal of contingent game experience is tied to a game's *mechanics.* Players often have to work together, whether they've just created a character or they're power players. From jumping into a group, having a healer remove diseases or wounds, getting temporary power through a dance at the local cantina, even selling raw materials and manufactured goods to other players, much is designed. Developers, for instance, put a great deal of thought into how the mechanical interface will support or restrict how people can talk. Within near every major online video game, players can see who else is online and send quick text messages. Whether or not a player began the game with other friends, or as a way of keeping in touch with online friends, the interface is what can show them who is also playing, what they're doing, and how best to strike up conversation. As players discover more players, it becomes more and more likely that somebody will be online and willing to talk, should they log on. The more they get to know these players, play with them, and learn to enjoy their company, the more they've built their own incentive to play.

In games, a great deal of your social capital depends on how much mechanical power you have within the world; in some cases it can decide whether you're revered, hated, or ignored. A long time ago, in the Star Wars Galaxies universe, Jedi were usually able to kill many dozens of enemies at once. They were revered by their allies, hated by enemies and, for many mechanical reasons, rarely seen. Doctors with superior medication could make certain players far more powerful than those with the usual medication. Treating such players well helped to establish beneficial, powerful relationships. Putting time into these power mechanics often gives players inordinate advantages, sometimes at great cost to a player's time in the primary or secondary world.

Many times we wouldn't buy new games, take the time to learn them, or ultimately enjoy them, if other people weren't also committing their time and resources. Whether it's our real life friends, or the ones that we only meet inside games, some play purely because of people. The presence of people doesn't simply mix in some convoluted sense of reality. Giving a real person any sort of kindness, whether it's a neat item or help from a Jedi, can give them actual, real-world joy. By proxy it gives you a sense of pride. If instead it's your preference to take their items or destroy them with your Jedi, that also has a real effect.

The struggle for power mechanics often leads players to swear their allegiance to guilds, the sometimes many-hundred-strong player organizations in these games. Joining a guild with mechanical power is a top priority for many players in games like World of Warcraft, Dark Age of Camelot, or other commercial MMO games. Once a player reaches the maximum level or otherwise tops off their "basic abilities" and becomes a powerful character in their own right, it's standard that the only other way to reach higher power and status is through what's called the "endgame." Near always, the only way to get to the endgame is with a guild.

This has most notoriously been the case in Blizzard Entertainment's World of Warcraft, where anyone can get into second- or third-rate guilds, but only those in the elite can build connections needed to access the most coveted of power players. Advancing, at some point, stops being just about what you can do yourself. There are other forms of status that can become more important than your individual power.

First up is *reputation*, and a player with a slandered one is going to have a really hard time getting invited to all of the really good parties.[28] Addicted or not, players at a certain level of accomplishment have invested staggering amounts of time to get there — and if they want to keep progressing they'll have to be high up on the "pick me, pick me" list. Having a good reputation mostly means that people haven't heard anything bad about you. This is important, because sometimes new players will have opportunities to steal. They could do that, but word travels fast in these games, most especially among the distinguished guilds.

Trust is an essential component to this, because individuals within guilds have often spent a great deal of time developing their collective power, commonly through rare items, limited types of skills training, and so forth. They must trust that you will use mechanical power to benefit the guild before they honor you with that individual power. Often, once somebody picks up a very powerful item, or is selected for a limited training, it's theirs forever. There's no compunction and often no option to return this improved mechanical power. Trust is going beyond just whether a guild has heard bad things about you. Though game designs may shift away from this paradigm, expectations accompany trust. Prominent guild leaders in a number of games operate "guild banks." In the World of Warcraft, some carry a net worth which can reach into the tens, possibly even hundreds of thousands of U.S. dollars. On a heightened level of trust, certain players will be granted access to banks or storehouses. The stakes of trust can be high, in these instances. Guild bank robberies have been common, yet at times never reported. In some cases game developers wash their hands of the affair; the issue of trust is between the gamers. In others, they forbid certain types of sharing in the first place. Some players trust others to the point of sharing the use of their entire character or account, every scrap of individual mechanical power they have. Because almost all MMO games forbid account sharing in the first place, reporting the heist would only force the game's creators to also remove the duped player's account. The heretofore Wild West, unpoliced atmosphere to many secondary worlds makes these power societies as important and cohesive as they are.

Some players have years of real time and real cash invested; taking care of something like a guild bank takes *responsibility*. Even with small pieces of power, trust and responsibility are tied. As more power becomes entrusted to individual players, more is expected. Most often this is the expectation that someone will be online much of the time, though this isn't strictly the only responsibility expected of involved gamers. Maybe that's why so many people find these kinds of relationships suspect. Not only do players establish sizable expectations for the number of hours they or others should play, or be available to play, but in these situations, human beings are often objectified. A changing gamer begins to perceive another living person as just another "structural characteristic," just one more button that has to be pushed for them to win. When that structural characteristic doesn't perform sufficiently, whether due to a lack of a good gaming computer, sleep, or anything else in the primary or secondary worlds, reputation and trust diminish. When the "structural characteristic" simply doesn't show up, there's usually no reasoning that will keep that reputation and trust from taking a major hit, whether the person needed to eat a meal, spend time with their children, or anything else. Not only is it shocking to what degree otherwise compassionate gamers objectify one another, but perhaps more shocking are the degrees to which they do it to themselves. There are various levels of severity here; very often the most mechanically powerful players have learned to avoid individuals who put the game before people. All the same, some familiarity with the mindset tends to be required for reaching that high-end level. Interacting socially can require some mechanical power. Having mechanical power requires some social interaction.

Though much of the social embedding in these games is mechanical, as designed and contrived as one might expect in any other single-player game, the simple presence of flesh-and-blood humans can make parts of the game unplanned and unplannable.[29] In one regard, the same easy agency that improves a single-player experience adds spontaneity to players looking to find and relate to new players. Players can seek out the kinds of relationships that have nothing to do with power, or the quality of someone's "gear." The randomness inherent to social interaction is one of the few things which helps the texture of online worlds get so close to the texture one might expect in reality.[30] It's extramechanical, which is to say that design has little or nothing to do with it. Online communication, let alone the kinds that players get in games, is unique. Though there's a physical distance, for many different reasons that can foster a psychological closeness not always found if one happens to live in a closed-off society. What's interesting with communication that can't be planned for, designed, or sometimes even anticipated is that players' actions very often loop back, changing the fundamentals of how the game was designed to work. When a significant number of the players you might find in these MMO games have access to programs for telephone-quality voice chat, the arguments about "antisocial gamers" could almost evaporate. Many of the gamers at the high end of the game have the information needed to access at least two or three such voice chat "servers," which contain many different "channels," the voice chat equivalent of a chat room. Though the psychological closeness or "emotional bandwidth" possible in an online environment has been praised by some and thought of as nonexistent by others, hearing the voices of living people can foster a specific kind of relationship. Close, with no strings attached. You can talk about what you want, when you want and vanish forever should you so choose.

While many, if not most, of the large guilds are about power, some others aren't about results; the occasional person joins simply so that he can enjoy people and keep in touch with friends. Not every guild in every game is about progressing to ever-more spectacular and imposing goals. Good online friends can value things besides the power of a person's sword, armor and items. People in the more social guilds often have *respect* for someone's personality, instead of how much wealth they have, or purely what they can do for a guild. Feelings of respect can sometimes come from things like reputation, trust and responsibility, though players meeting socially, within or outside a guild, can also get *emotional support* for their real-world successes, failures, and challenges. Strong friendships don't usually emerge instantaneously, they're grown. Whether over voice chat, personal conversations, or group banter, oftentimes players in online games brag, joke, and seek advice from people. Sometimes this emotional growth is aided by *recognition*, often by gaining actual levels of rank in a guild. Whereas a lot of the elite and goal-oriented guilds have to take on inconvenient responsibilities when they're promoted, promotion within a social group usually just means that people like you better. Or that you've done a better job avoiding drama.

Though some players can accumulate a great deal of power within the game's mechanical structure and still be human beings, it can be a challenge for others. There are lines that can be crossed, not only in whether a gamer's primary life suffers from being drawn into the secondary, but in how they begin to view people. In reality it's easy for most people to recognize that other humans have feelings and needs. But in games bandied as a consumer entertainment, people pay to have an experience. Sometimes they pay for the opportunity to help and encourage others. Sometimes they, as Kateri puts it, "cut throats." One final element of motivation may explain more as to why.

This Is Your Brain

"I was literally, in a movie-esque moment, looking in the bathroom mirror and wondering what I had become." Andrew originally wrote the blog post that we discussed earlier, recounting his ill-fated journey through the World of Warcraft. Before any of it he remembers being the spontaneous type, rallying all of his friends to a party on Tuesday night, a self-proclaimed "bar king." While friends in the primary, real world came and went in Warcraft for relationships and the story, he took on the responsibility of helping to lead a guild. As people in his guild began looking to the game less for friendship or light entertainment and more for in-game power, material rewards, and the hardcore play, he found himself changing with them. "I created a conflict," he says, "Sorry, 'it' created a conflict. I have always been an empathetic person, pretty outgoing. When I got into the guild, it was like a whole new pool of people to meet and learn from. As this group of people turned more towards achievement inside the game, the expectations went through the roof. I found I was playing all the time; all the while my intense playing was alienating all of my other friends in the real world.

As the playing became more intense, so did the drive for gratification. "Everyone wanted everything right away, and I got stuck in the sticky middle. I was the cream in Satan's Oreo. I, like thousands of others, let my personal life and my 'character' intertwine too much. When you become addicted to something there is a need, a craving that needs to be filled. At first," he recalls, "there was never really a need for that space. I had a lot of outside friends and family who I saw a lot."

The way that the game was designed clashed with the person Andrew had been before he started playing. He explains, "You get locked into the mechanics of the character you portray. I was never Andy the engineer or Andy the DJ or Andy the friend; I was Ampren the mage."

Andrew has changed a lot in the three years since seeing himself again, his epiphany with the mirror. He's engaged, settled into his job, and shares that one of the things he's taken from his time in Warcraft is "an appreciation for the real world" and for the people in it. He's still outgoing, explaining, "It's one thing to put people first, but it has to be the right people. I can't spend every single day and night worrying about a video game. It doesn't matter your reasonings, when you spend that much time concentrating on something, you run the risk of becoming one-dimensional."

And games can change the brain, making it one-dimensional. When we're young, so much of the brain is changing, growing skills and grasping emotions, that it used to be thought the brain could really only change during childhood. Through more recent advancements in how the brain changes, or brain plasticity, we've found that the human brain is constantly re-tooling itself and re-envisioning what it's capable of. Though we get more into how this works during the chapter on kids and gaming, for now it's enough to say that Andrew is right. Spending all of your time doing one thing, be it video games, filling out TPS reports, or anything else, the human brain literally can become one-dimensional.

In a longtime, heavy gamer, building up skill at living and interacting inside a digital world is part and parcel with being a "good gamer," somebody who understands how to play. Given how much of that play in an online secondary world takes specific kinds of reflexes, muscle memory and thinking, even just for proper immersion and a basic understanding of how to act in-game, we have to assume that these skills are being locked into the brain.

To bring up Andrew's case, playing a mage in the game World of Warcraft, it can be incredibly easy to get locked into the unique things one has to do in order to play a successful mage. You warp all over the place, freeze enemies into place, cast specific spells at specific times. Even within Warcraft, that one specific game, the way a mage might train his brain could be completely different from the way a warrior or a priest might train his. During even just one year of playing four to fourteen hours a day, which is becoming more commonplace internationally, the brain will learn these patterns of thought with surprising, even alarming efficiency. Depending on how much of his primary life a gamer trades in, and for how long at a time, this can possibly leave other neural pathways to degrade. Even simple things can suffer, like acting and reacting in social situations, how to write, play music, or engage in sports that the gamer had enjoyed in the past.

These changes tend not to happen lightly, nor do they happen without our brain's silent approval. Even having agency, let alone having personal and social experiences within games which carry one beyond what's available in reality, can encourage the brain. Even completely healthy people sometimes have a hard time sorting out subtle chemical motivations from their tangible reasonings for doing something. A gamer might think to himself, "I'm logging on so that I can hang out with Rob!" That might be a slice of the motivational pie, but chances are that he's being driven by much more.

As it happens, the thinking that we use to justify decisions will sometimes, if not usually, have no connection to what's really driving action. Our reasoning is tacked on afterward, partly because parts of our brains can react more quickly than other parts can think about and understand those reactions. The brain remembers rewarding actions. It seeks out those actions. Some of this has to do with health. With good physical and mental health, it becomes easier to realize when we're feeling a nonsensical pull to something like a video game. We scrunch up our faces, look at the computer monitor or the television screen, and say, "Hah! I don't think so, Mr. Brain! I have to be at work in an hour, and I'm not ready yet!" Other times, especially if giving in to these urges has gotten pretty common, we tack on reasonings that might not be completely honest. "I'm just logging in for five minutes, just to see if I sold that intergalactic death ray."

In many cases the brain is more likely to release dopamine, one of the key brain chemicals when it comes to motivating us to go and do something. Dopamine is cited in research on all addictions, whether to drugs or gambling; it is one of the few chemicals that we're sure motivates people. Discovered all but by accident, it's become a buzzword. Some of the researchers looking at video games go so far as to say that when we game, dopamine is released.[31] So games have to be addictive, right? Dopamine is being released, after all.

We can get a little bit more specific than that. Our brains learn to release more dopamine when certain experiences are *readily available* and *easy to get*. When we have a lot of different satisfying experiences that are pretty much at our fingertips, like poping Halo 3 into the X-box, that's good availability. In games like World of Warcraft, it's been made easy to grab a friend and battle other players. After we've picked out the media experience that we want, the next question is whether that experience gives us what we want easily enough. That's the essence of what separates good from failed game design. Good games provide the illusion that a player's accomplishments were insurmountable feats, the stuff of poetry and legend, when in fact every one of the player's successes and victories were planned. In other words, games strive to make the rewards easier than plucking a microwaveable dinner from a local supermarket. The difficulty of nearly everything in contemporary life is being constantly eased. Procuring food becomes faster. The food appears to be more nutritious. Traveling over oceans no longer takes weeks to accomplish and months of salary. With the internet, you don't even have to physically meet a sexual partner before making plans to have sex. In some senses of the word, things are easier.

In light of these trends everywhere else in the world, secondary worlds designed for pure pleasure don't seem so anomalous. It's fairly normal for a technological advancement to give us all of our feelings of achievement and satisfaction in one easy, targeted sitting. Going into the same game all the time can be called a lot of different things: feedback, quality, addiction. The fact is that the same principles which guide "good game design" also coincide with what we know about the chief chemical known to affect motivation and addiction. In a way that's perhaps indirect, good game design is equivalent to addictive game design. Whether or not it registers on a conscious level, gamers will want the stimulation from meeting goals in video games. Their brains will tell them that it's a good idea. Without education as to how immersion works and the different ways in which the experience attracts, for game developers, gamers and society in general, many gamers will not be able to stop. It may be that nobody is to blame, if much of this comes out of natural reactions to a new form of experience, like immersion. But having someone to blame wouldn't miraculously release the waylaid gamers. These people would still be locked into an experience, oftentimes not having the first idea why they're playing. Contrasting the perceptions of many gamers and designers, that what's being created is fun, with the perceptions of parents, spouses, doctors and non-gaming society, that certain games are an unshakable vortex of addiction, what are we left with? An overdose of fun? What other features in today's highest-grossing games cause this?

Maressa Orzack, Ph.D., is an assistant clinical professor at Harvard Medical School who founded a hospital-based treatment program for computer addiction. She has stated that game designers carefully orchestrate principles of behavioral psychology within games in order to create addiction. Dr. Orzack identifies the process of character progression and the in-game reward system as one aspect of operant conditioning, intentionally being structured into games. Stating that forty percent of MMORPG players show signs of addiction, she goes so far as to state, "The MMORPG is an addictive drug that needs to be regulated." Orzack should be able to recognize operant conditioning when she sees it; during her years of early training she worked with the groundbreaking behavioral psychologist B.F. Skinner, the originator of the formal theory of operant conditioning in the 1950s and 1960s.[32] The tenets of operant conditioning are simple. Gamers can easily recognize them in games, where they're referred to as the dings, the little rewards that we get. Skinner viewed human motivation and resulting behavior as a very simple system of reinforcement, extinction, and punishment. A reinforcer is easily understood as a reward one gets for a desired behavior. A punishment is something designed to stop a specific behavior. Extinction is when a behavior is ignored — neither rewarded nor punished — and eventually stops on its own. Obviously, behaviors which result in rewards occur most frequently.

Skinner developed his theory by experiments conducted with what is now called the Skinner Box. A rat or pigeon confined in a box would be rewarded with food pellets for pressing the lever a certain number of times and in certain patterns. By using different patterns of reinforcement, Skinner was able to get the rat to press the lever almost continuously. The principles of the Skinner Box have been creatively adapted by game developers who understand the ding principle and have taught us that there are certain ways to arrange goals which make it far more likely that video game players will keep coming back. Rewards are given in video games on a near continuous basis, through the gaining of experience points (xp) which allow for your character to level regularly. At first, most games hand out these first rewards like some grandparents give out cookies and candy. It's a lot of sweets and they're usually pretty good. In the game, every action performed, any little thing that you do, gives you one of these rewards: Kill a bunny, get shiny new swords and armor; developing skills, powers, and various other attributes—it's like giving a puppy a hunk of beef every time he urinates on the newspaper instead of on the couch. In the stereotypical good game, these rewards all carry the false illusion of difficulty, juxtaposed with a reward that looks an awful lot like that juicy hunk of meat does to the dog. Contrast this with something a dog doesn't have to worry much about: that pesky, complex thing called reality. If in real life you kill some wandering rabbit, all you have is a dead bunny body, a guilty conscience and some lucky feet. In the game world, the bunny body mystically fades away, leaving you with gold, jewels, treasure, and the foundations of a bold new experience. Killing that bunny prepares you for dastardly villains and virulent dragons.

These are rewards that the brain likes. The part of your brain that thinks about the world probably understands that destroying adorable creatures may not be a foundational life experience. Another part says, "Ah, gold. Gold good." These reinforcers encourage a person to keep playing. Kill enough fluffy bunnies and you can afford a better weapon and new piece of armor, meaning you become immediately more powerful, can kill more stuff, go more places, see new things, meet new people, complete quests, all of which open the door to more reinforcement.

But then something a little tricky happens. The reinforcement system starts to slow down. You have to kill bigger, meaner monsters to earn the xp, the money, and the gear. You don't level so fast. This is where a lot of people find they start to want to play longer and work harder, because they've already been conditioned to want the dings that go with having the stuff. Killing the bunnies doesn't earn you any xp; you need to kill stallions for that next level. And dang it all, stallions don't die as quickly! You want to play with your other friends in the game, but you can't do that unless you are up to their level! Since you can't play with these cool kids until you've gotten high enough in level, you're stuck with the stallions. What's happened from the standpoint of behavioral psychology is that the schedule of reinforcement has changed. You're no longer getting a ding for every little thing you do.

One developer anonymously remarked, "We make it just like gambling. Sometimes you get something, sometimes you don't. When you get something it's really exciting, so you want to keep at it because you antic-ipate it might be the very next time you complete a quest or kill a certain mob, you'll get something really cool." The designer has done a bait and switch. While your brain was getting used to the consistent, juicy rewards of those first few levels, the designers slowly started to introduce a pattern of intermittent reinforcement. Though a blitzkrieg of positive reinforce-ment is nice and all, intermittent reinforcement is the most powerful way to keep people engaged in a repetitive activity. It even allows them to tol-erate the occasional punishment, another effective way for a designer to control behavior.

Different games punish in various ways. The punishment usually hap-pens when your character dies and has to go through some sort of labo-rious process to come back to life in the same place he or she or it was before. In some games, xp is lost with every death, setting a player back hours or days of time. Sometimes valuable gear is lost — dropped — with every death. When a player has experienced a punishment, it's a big incen-tive to not die again *and* to work hard right away to earn back the lost xp and dropped stuff. It's also incentive to become a more skilled player and learn how to stay alive. Even though punishment sucks, in the game world, it's structured as an incentive to work *harder* and stick with the game *longer*.

After all, once you've made friends in the game, you have to keep up with their leveling process and their level of mechanical power or you can't play with them. And you like your friends. Many of the cooler things in secondary worlds can't be done by one gamer alone. Your friends reward you by asking you to play with them, by helping you in your different quests, and you all help each other to level faster, get better stuff, and see the more dangerous locations. You achieve, which is a reward. You achieve a lot more with your friends. You have to play as much as they do, and some of them may play a whole lot. Now your friends offer you reinforce-ment for playing. They may be angry at you and critical if you don't play — a form of punishment. Social embedding, in many ways, becomes a form of social conditioning.

With the many social requirements to obtaining the best rewards, along with the many chance rewards that come purely from socialization, game experiences can distinguish themselves from the primary world in one more critical way. People who can work effectively in this high-reward environment, who can train their bodies to effectively achieve with other specific players, learn an almost tribal cohesion. Considered by some to be the father of modern social sciences, in the later 1300s Muslim scholar Ibn Khaldun put to pen a theory for how history functions. To oversimplify it, he noted that communication and cohesion among desert warriors was such that they would band together to conquer the cities. Then, building culture and growing fat themselves, after many generations they would become the cities, ripe pickings for a new desert people. The heightened communication and cohesion of the desert people is the most interesting part of his theory, for our purposes.

The desert was unforgiving. The punishment was starvation, disease or worse. Games, in an odd sense, are also unforgiving. The "punishment," to speak outside Skinner's terms, is to be denied the higher, more coveted reinforcers. It's not fearing death that demands people to work seamlessly with one another so much as suffering the absence of fun. In games there may not be the real punishment of the desert, but rather failure to maximize positive reinforcement.

In this light, it's not hard to imagine why some guilds build enough solidarity to actually keep people together when they go *between* different games. When starting from scratch, some move like tribes, sticking with the same people for years on end. It's interesting to consider that while most non-gamers wouldn't pick up something so time-consuming on the advice of a few dozen people that they'd never met face to face, many gamers abandon those who were once real-life friends for those whom they trust to bring on the fun.[33]

Can we call this "the communication of fun," or at this point does it become something else? It may be a personal thing, of where somebody's line is, though in many ways such relationships and rewards reach extremes. Some, as you'll see in the following chapter, come very close to mimicking the workings of addiction.

On a neurobiological level, brain changes are happening when people experience reinforcement for specific behaviors. Evidence suggests that our wily old neurotransmitter for pleasure, dopamine, is activated by even subtle reinforcements, creating new neural pathways that lead to structural changes in the brain. Rewards don't just have to be easy to get and readily available if they've been packaged right. Chances are good that secondary worlds can change the human brain in multiple ways. Many of these are going to keep people playing, whether or not they actually enjoy the game. The rewards are structured into the media experience in a complex, multi-layered way. There's always something new to do, more rewards to achieve, more people to play with. New dings are everywhere. In essence, the game becomes a perpetual rush. In a society oriented toward commercial gain that might make great consumer sense. The problem is that these *are* experiences, whose rewards are nothing like real life.

In real life, we don't consistently get dings for every activity we do. We often have to work hard at things for long periods of time, and we don't get immediate rewards for it. Sometimes we don't get rewards at all. One of the main criticisms of operant conditioning methods is that while people may respond to the system, they actually become dependent upon receiving external rewards in order to feel motivated. A person who is initially motivated by their own intrinsic reasons for achieving may become dependent on these outside rewards and actually lose their innate internal motivation to achieve things in life. This happens. Current and former gamers often express surprising levels of frustration in common and formerly easy real-life situations. It might be fair to ask whether some gamers' brains are locked into these patterns of powerful rewards, both constant and random. And none of this begins to touch on the fact that people are basically being manipulated to do things on deep levels, usually below their conscious level of awareness. There's no disclaimer on the game box stating, "By playing this game your brain may be changed in ways that will affect your moods and motivations in ways that ultimately may not be in your own best interest. You risk addiction and may lose control of your ability to function in work, school, or interpersonal relationships." The game companies don't care — at least, they don't care yet. There's money to be made in keeping up the subscription base with as little new content as possible. Pushing the envelope, creating imaginative, challenging and thoughtful content, is the exception. The unfortunate majority of developers have become masters at the art of building the dinging rat maze. These traditional games can be repeated indefinitely, making for an exceptional return on investment.

If we consider the factors at work in operant conditioning methods, it's easy to see how the grind inherent in many games is similar to that rat in the box. And when the immersive qualities of media experience are added, people become socially embedded; when a biological, addictive process is thrown into the mix, it's easy to understand how many people lose sense of their primary lives.

Four

ANATOMY OF A
GAME ADDICTION

Sometimes gamers are playing for fun, but sometimes it's because their brains and bodies are telling them that they have to. It isn't going to happen to every gamer, and it certainly won't show up overnight. Games are complicated, and a *lot* is happening when a player physically cannot stop playing. If any one thing were causing these problems, it would be ignorance. Almost nobody understands enough about games or themselves to keep their play balanced. Games give gamers exactly what they want, when they want it: For many that's an easy pill to swallow. But as long as we're talking about pills, let's make one point abundantly clear: games are not drugs.[1] Cute names like "WarCrack" and "EverCrack" might be funny, but drugs (crack included) all work in specific ways.[2] Heroin mimics our body's natural opiates, meaning almost instantaneous and intense feelings of sedation and satisfaction.[3] Alcohol goes to work in a few different parts of the brain, slowing transmitters called GABA and flooding parts of the brain with glutamate.[4] All of these real drugs, from meth and morphine to cocaine and ecstasy, affect brain chemistry *after* they've been ingested, injected or otherwise introduced into the system. Games aren't injecting substances into a gamer's fingers whenever they type. Players could do drugs while they play, which would change things, but games aren't drugs in and of themselves.

So what about behavioral addictions? For the last few decades we've tagged all sorts of different behaviors as potentially addictive, like running, sex, and eating salty foods.[5] These still release certain chemicals, but they're the chemicals that we humans get from everyday experience. A binge eater might be ingesting foot-long club sandwiches, but it's the chemicals being unleashed by the brain and body that are doing the satisfying. Drug and alcohol addictions are usually also part behavioral addiction, but that's over and above whatever specific things a substance is doing in the brain.[6] It's why some people can kick a drug habit, but they still get nostalgic around their favorite countryside crack house.

While games are still just experiences, those experiences have been designed to be as rewarding as possible. Game addictions are behavioral addictions on steroids, so to speak. The gaming experience has been intimately and carefully designed to make gamers think that they're doing these huge, difficult deeds. They're not. The game designers actually did most of the work that went into fabricating that illusion.[7] It can take hundreds of specialized professionals to do the fabricating for newer games. Gaming starts out as legitimate, sure, but it also floods the brain and body with a lot more stimulation than most other legitimate behaviors in the world.[8]

Games make it easy for us to fulfill deep and spectacular desires. On Earth, somebody who can't get enough of a certain real behavior might face limitations: a running addict might eventually reach exhaustion; a drug addict might run out of money; an adrenaline junkie might wreck the car. Technology eases and sometimes altogether removes those limits. Obviously, someone who loves spending money might learn to avoid a few impediments online and a voyeur can spy on plenty of people with the aid of YouTube, MySpace, or one of the tens of thousands of live porn sites online. What happens inside a secondary, video game world can go beyond the regular laws of physics and the normal progression of time. Once players enter, they're playing inside worlds made to woo them. Achieving knightly deeds is made easy. Just as easy as stealing cars and running over hookers, in fact. They aren't limited to getting just one or two kinds of chemical excitements for doing deeds inside these illusionary worlds. Their minds suck in the experience, one where the daunting and dangerous takes only a few quick key clicks.[9]

Video games aren't drugs, but rather a heightened and idealized experience. They aren't unique in this respect. Every media experience, every story and television show, will try to make events more intense and pleasurable than what we're used to in reality. As time goes by, television has been consistently outdoing itself in rehashing sex and violence.[10] Games aren't really unique here; sexy, violent games sell the best. We can't wonder why they get made the most. While society tends to agree that enjoying entertainment is legitimate, there comes a point where things fall out of balance. Though video games that encourage long and intense sessions are going to invite trouble, game addiction isn't ever an event. It's almost always a slow-moving process.[11]

More Than Enough

Meet Rick Pendlebury, a gamer's gamer from the United Kingdom. He balances games, work, relationships, World of Warcraft, and even human conversation "without breaking into a sweat." Rick has been playing since he was five; in every game that he mentions, he remembers something unique. Rick's love of gaming is a lot more complex than a rat suckling on a nicotine dispenser. "Up, Down, Left, Right; put your finger on A and press Start, which was the level select cheat," he recalls, like a Freemason reciting some secret code of membership. "Sonic the Hedgehog was colorful, fast-paced and had a catchy tune." After buying over a dozen different game systems and upgrading his computer "God knows how many times," Rick has picked up the games that spoke to him. Games with a sense of humor, visual and artistic beauty, games that speak to his love of travel and exploration, that enchant his mind with vivid characters and deep back story, that let him mentor younger players and bring in friends. He's in a place to say, "It's just a game," and has humor enough to laugh when his roommate asks, "How are things in 'The World?'" At the same time, he understands the draw on a practical level. "The more I played it, the more I mastered it and so the more I craved it."

Like a lot of players, Rick understands a good deal of what he's looking for in the gaming experience. Although he puts his craving for games in roughly the same ballpark as a nicotine addiction, he knows how to balance things.

"I can put things into perspective," he says, grinning. "It's just that Warcraft comes quite high in that ranking."

Games can very naturally climb that ranking. For gamers like Rick, a video game offers "just enough." It's just the right amount of fun and satisfaction, making video games a sometimes genuine addition to his life (he's since put down Warcraft, for the time being). For others, games provide a bit more than enough. Some of the things that we do in reality are inherently rewarding, but some are just plain tedious. The tedious parts, unfortunately, are usually the ones that feed us, clothe us, and keep the human race in control of an uncontrollable world. Fun and satisfying experiences give us reliable chemical rewards, which can make them appear more attractive than the necessities, the proverbial crop-planting and child-raising. A constant for humans is that once we can see good and reliable short-term rewards, it can be easy to begin taking our first small steps in building a very large problem.

In the last few years, neurologists have greatly advanced our knowledge of how brain chemistry creates motivation.[12] Beyond just how rewards are scheduled, which we briefly mentioned earlier, our brains are always on the lookout for good short-term rewards or reliable long-term rewards.[13] If we pick a tasty yellow banana from a tree, take a nibble, and experience no heartburn or indigestion, then cool. The brain is going to give us the thumbs up. If the banana is overpoweringly scrumptious, then the brain will probably want another one. Our brains are always collecting information about what they're experiencing out in the world and things that provide more satisfaction, more quickly, are going to look more appealing to our brains. If we can get as many of these magic bananas as we want, whenever we want, then our brains are going to get pretty used to having them around. This is because goal-oriented motivation, or in this case banana-oriented motivation, is based on two major factors: the availability of reward and the effort required to obtain it.[14] If we get used to eating these magical bananas over a fairly long period of time, and they never stop being the most enjoyable part of our day, then eating them is going to be higher on our list than some other things. Any given person is going to have a fairly long to-do list, a mental list of things that they like doing.[15] Some people like to talk on the phone, other people like to sail boats, still other people might like watching some television. On a deep level our mind tends to rate those based on whether they'll get us what we want. Many people, much of the time, aren't aware of this ordering. If talking to Sally on the phone is at the top of their list, then they might give that a try first. If they can't get ahold of Sally, then they might try to go sail in their boat.

94

If they can't do that, then they'll just watch some television. Television is a nice fallback for a lot of people. Plenty of channels, doesn't take much effort, and occasionally something good is on. A bit like our magical banana, it's got that combination of available, easy-to-get stimulation. So long as there's something good on.

Back to the hypothetical banana, if our to-eat list includes rice, then bread, then peanuts, and yet there's always a fresh supply of these curiously delicious bananas, then at some point eating them can easily become our number one choice. It's always dependable, always satisfying, and therefore it becomes an obvious choice every time. If we *keep* eating bananas with no regard to anything else, we might reach a point where other foods just don't match up. It becomes a chore to eat the rice, the bread, the peanuts, and everything else that supports healthy nutrition.

Games offer more than something tasty. Many of today's players have spent countless hours going from game to game, so they know when to move to a better experience. They know how to get the kind of stimulation that they want. Even with people who haven't played many games, remember that well-designed games make it easy for them to learn how to get something that they'll like.[16]

MMO games, like World of Warcraft, can sometimes provide so many different options that a person doesn't need to go between games.[17] This might look like the following. "If nobody shows up for the raid, then I'll do my laundry. If there aren't any laundry machines open, then I might log back on and quest to save Peetey the Pirate. Unless my friend Paco is online. If Paco is online I'll probably play all night." At some point, sitting down at a computer gives you an entire world of things to do. All games go above and beyond our magical banana. Playing inside a game feels real; it's designed to be better than reality and it's always around. Games, especially of the MMO variety, are uniquely capable of topping our to-do list.

A behavior can sit, harmless, at or near the top of someone's list. It can sit there for a while. If it elevates itself over the others, then Houston, we have a problem. When this happens, problem gamers can start to sacrifice other behaviors that used to bring them a lot of short- and long-term happiness. They might take them out in snippets or in large chunks, but they make sure that they're spending less time on those other behaviors.

95

They've got to have more time for their favorite, after all. After enough of this light pruning, some behaviors get taken off of the list entirely. This is called a motivational monopoly. The person has lost the taste for other things, because they simply don't provide as much excitement, relaxation, or satisfaction as the one domineering behavior.

Motivational monopolies are serious, but they tend not to appear overnight. Video games can give a lot of people a lot of different reasons to play, but to reach the point of addiction they have to be played. A lot. When people play video games for more hours each day, and more days each week, these media experiences become a bigger part of their lives. As gamers take more and more of these small steps in the wrong direction, cutting out pieces of their primary world, their ability to feel more comfortable in a game has the room it needs to grow. With fewer chemically appealing reasons to be in the primary world, the brain is left with the impression that the game world is just a better place to be. Remember that this is the *brain's* impression.

Any behavior that starts down this path is literally growing on some-body; it's changing how the brain and body works.[18] Journeying from game to game, gamers learn to use certain forms of the digital living room more effectively. The joysticks and keyboards always work a little bit differently, but all the brain needs is to figure out how to use them. That knowledge is being imprinted in the brain, and little by little good games are going to be giving the brain just the right kudos and congratulations for that learning. Games are fun to learn, and playing better usually means more powerful rewards are getting to the brain.

Said another way, the brain becomes sensitized, or sensitive to what games have to offer. The more a gamer's brain becomes sensitized to one game, the higher that game can in turn crank up the brain's pleasure dial. Sometimes this means that the gamer is getting thrills from the action, or smug satisfaction from winning, but it doesn't have to be any one thing. All they really know is that if they go into game X, and then do Y or Z, then they're going to feel how they want to feel. Often they won't really know what feelings they crave — they're just drawn to the game when the brain wants more.[19]

When a gamer is getting these cravings, very different chemicals, not to mention experiences, could be responsible. Some gamers could be adrenaline junkies. They live for the excitement of certain games. If they get really pumped up with Dance Dance Revolution, or maybe a gunfighter game, then their brains can start to get used to being pumped up on adrenaline all of the time. If you really do have an adrenaline junkie on your hands, then that may mean that the next game, television show, or street race is going to have to be just a little more intense than the last. If it isn't, then they're liable to not even notice the excitement — only that they feel a bit more normal.

The rewards and fulfillments in video games are also likely to sensitize us to another chemical, one that we've pointed to a few times as being a key to motivation. More and more, dopamine has been studied in relation to motivation, but also all of the different addictions to behaviors. Dopamine works in a few different parts of the brain to do a lot of different things; one of these is to reward us for a behavior that has powerful payoffs. When games sensitize our brain to most any kind of rewarding feeling, the brain is learning how to get more and more of the stimulation that it wants. Today's games tend to revolve around experiences that get us excited, or make us feel good because we're learning something new, connecting with people, or getting the opportunity to do things that'd be impossible in reality.[20] While these different behaviors might not always push the same buttons in the brain, getting what we want is going to release dopamine. If a game experience is flooding the brain with dopamine, that means every other experience in life, on our to-do list, can begin to look less satisfying by comparison.

If our brains reach the point where they're more sensitized to the rewards of a secondary game world than to those in reality, then games are naturally going to displace everything else on our to-do list. We humans are built to grab at the things which are most consistent with rewarding our brains. If somebody fails to control the urge to play, with the result being that they sacrifice primary, real world behaviors, then their brains won't stop changing. If they keep playing video games, especially after the digital living room has become the only thing that can effectively get them excited or happy, then their brains can begin to rewire themselves. Gamers at this stage understand games better than they do the real world, reality makes less sense.

If you've ever been, or been around, the gamer for whom walking and talking is a challenge, it could very well be that their skills have migrated. It can be helpful to think of games as limbs, like we discussed earlier in the book.[21] When players get used to using computers as their eyes and ears inside a game world, their bodies won't want to up and amputate that limb without a struggle. It's the same with people who have gotten used to using the internet to get information; part of what an addict gets in these worlds is an experience of something beyond themselves.[22] At this point gamers have tuned their senses to be more efficient players, sometimes to the detriment of being able to act and interact in the primary world.[23]

While this process tends to take a lot of time, certain games are notorious for grabbing hold of gamers *very* quickly and *very* effectively. MMO games are approaching the texture of everyday life, making them feel more real and visceral.[24] They also reward players for spending more time inside the world. The more they're online, the better they can contribute to the groups that are looking to get things done.[25] Once they get a few of those things done, they'll be better equipped to fight more powerful monsters and reach prominent status.[26] There's almost always a reason to increase the amount of time they spend playing. Anyone can get used to treating these secondary worlds just like they might a real place, because in many respects they are real places.[27] These places are increasingly in direct competition with the rest of reality. Most of the entertainment we've had in human history gives us natural breaking points: The chapter ends, the film ends, or there's a commercial break. It gives us an opportunity to rest and use the bathroom, and in general it lets our attention return to the primary world. If a break lets us suddenly realize that we're late for work, then we can panic, get in the car, and drive to work. In games, the basic model of human body isn't the least bit skilled at breaking away.[28] In fact, sometimes gamers don't notice the loud noises and rabid dogs in the room. Unless real-life distractions actually knock a gamer out of his chair, those distractions usually just get tuned out and forgotten.[29] With games that don't provide natural breaking points, gamers might not realize that they skipped work until after their shift is over. Though game addictions tend to build in small steps, someone who plays for twelve hours in one day is going to start to take those steps at a much faster pace.

Stephen King once wrote that the purpose of art was to serve life, not the other way around.[30] As more forms of entertainment start to take on the features of games, we as consumers will have to insist on creative new tools to regulate ourselves. When somebody reaches the point of motivational monopoly, he isn't using media to recuperate and recharge. It's not about enjoying a medium for the skill of the artist behind it. It's about giving the brain a powerful jolt — which could be dulling the taste for reality. This isn't happening just because some gamers are sloppy and irresponsible; it's the consequence of having spaces that are rewarding and real-feeling. Until now only a few people have completely lost themselves in things like books or television, so not too many folks have taken the time to understand why.

Taking Care of Business

Game addiction takes an addict, but that's not a topic that invites easy self-exploration. For gamers, it's partially the problem of facing the demons that make them play. I played partly to face the embarrassment of not having many vile demons to speak of. The ease of slipping into a game, demons or no, baffles the best of us.

In high school, somebody close to me began suffering from a serious string of drug addictions. She was sent to an international rehab center, so in order to understand the process I attended an affiliated group therapy program. Surrounded by alcoholics, hardcore drug addicts, and your standard dysfunctional people, it was time to share our demons, put them on the table. Someone asked, "What's *your* problem, Nails?" (My name gets mispronounced a lot.) "Well," I started, "It's not life-threatening or anything, but I get caught up in playing video games. There are times when my days just vanish."

It took a while for the eighty people in the room to stop laughing, even the Tony Robbins wannabe. Rather than entertain the thought that a computer could cause problems, the psychologist leading the session spoke for the crowd. "Games," he scoffed, "games don't cause problems, Nayls. Are you sure that you don't have any real problems?" He listed off some examples, like alcohol or past molestation.

Is that what they really expected? "Oh, you guys know everything!

99

Of *course* I was molested! Silly me to try pulling one over on the masters of psychology!" Sure, sixteen-year-old Neils had your usual teen problems: Nobody at his high school wanted to be his girlfriend, the teachers of his favorite subjects were comically terrible and his voice still cracked. While that group therapy temporarily took me past some basic issues of confidence (molestation commentary notwithstanding), the problem of playing too much was never resolved.

Since games weren't something that I could balance on my own; they continued to create other "real" issues. A few years down the road, probably my second year in college, life was slipping through my fingers. I was playing games in order to escape the stress of... Not being able to stop playing games. Maybe I was destined to build some kind of addiction regardless, but I do wish that I'd had some help at regulating myself. Today, my love of games is all too often spoilt by the issues they bring up. I don't want that.

Gamers don't always need help to start playing for the wrong reasons, but nothing helps like a sprinkling of our standard human tragedies, uncertainties and failures. The individual is an essential element, but it's almost never as simple as having an "addictive personality." There are a host of different reasons, psychological, genetic or otherwise, that can drive certain individuals to pursue specific games, substances, or other behaviors.[31] On top of that, isolated events can pop up and trigger binging. Even subtle frustrations can prompt seemingly innocuous escapism. Eventually some gamers reach the tipping point, where a game has been played too much and for too long. As video games overtake reality, the problems stack up.

One of the biggest pieces of addiction has to do with how you deal with those problems. Your ability to function can make one of the single largest contributions either to staving off or inviting a more desperate situation. Life functioning refers to how well we are doing in several basic areas of life: the job, the schoolwork, the quality of relationships with family and friends. It starts with the basics: hygiene, grooming, nutrition, exercise, and sleep. The more these things go away, the more you can say that something is wrong on a common-sense level.

To function well in life you need at least three basic skills: being aware of yourself, being able to monitor yourself, and being able to change what you're doing when things get off-kilter. Taking care of your life is enormously easier when you, at the very least, understand the basics of these three self-skills. These are a simplified way to conceptualize self-regulation. They largely develop in childhood, though they can be remedially developed by adults who are adequately motivated. These three skills work together to fuel someone's ability to stay emotionally balanced and mentally healthy; they're the foundation for functioning, and problems in any one area can cause a domino effect.

People who are self-aware are conscious at all times of what they are feeling with their *emotions*, sensing in their *bodies*, and thinking in their *minds*. They can say fairly objectively whether they're doing things that are going to cause problems. Self-aware people recognize not only what is happening in the physical environment they are in, but also what is happening in the emotional environment of others around them. For all that, awareness is just about the present, what's happening in the here and now. Though it may sound like self-awareness is something that just happens for most people naturally, in reality many people are not very good at understanding their own emotions, how they think, and the state of their bodies. Unfortunately, not understanding yourself tends to mean that you'll also have a hard time understanding others.

Self-awareness is a skill that to a large extent is developed in childhood, when we start to associate words with our different feelings, like angry, happy, or discombobulated. Have you ever noticed that children and teens say that they're "bored" a lot? A large part of this is that it takes them time to discover and associate better words with other feelings, if they ever really learn them at all. If we're tuned in to our own feelings as well as to what we're thinking, then this opens the door to a better understanding of why we do what we do. We might know that gaming for six hours got us pumped, but we might also know that it made us feel other uncomfortable emotions.

Not all people develop enough self-awareness, because parents who aren't themselves self-aware can't help their kids to develop in that way. This results in people who walk through life in a state of partial awareness. They often experience unpleasant emotions and then do things to cope that aren't ultimately all that constructive. They often make choices that don't work out well, never quite knowing why.

Let's say that we're walking around in a chronic state of mild depression or anxiety, always having bad thoughts about ourselves. People in that situation might always be prone to unconsciously looking for things to make themselves feel better — without realizing that's what we're doing. Urges to binge eat, smoke, drink, watch hours of television — things we often consider to be bad habits or addictions — they often start when a person is uncomfortable but unaware. They make attempts to find something that makes them feel better, or at least helps them to feel numb. We call these attempts to escape *defense mechanisms*, though things like avoidance, denial and distraction keep us from understanding ourselves. Self-aware people think and act with insight, free to make willing decisions in their own best interests.

Self-monitoring takes that just a bit farther; it's being aware of the emotions, thoughts, and sensations that we've had in the past. Examining our actual behavior, certain patterns can start popping up. What situations, people, or objects trigger reactions within us? Sometimes monitoring your emotions over time is difficult, because there are a lot of mixed feelings. "Wow, I had a fight with John and went right home and got on the computer. I felt better after I logged in, but I started flirting with that wizard again. I promised myself I wouldn't do that any more. This pattern is making me feel like...."

Finally, self-correction means that, on our own, we can see the patterns and stop them. Self-correction is taking independent action when we notice that we've done something that isn't helping us, actually sets us back, or at worst is hurting somebody around us or ourselves. The person who can self-correct doesn't need someone else to tell them what to do. Basic self-correction for a functioning gamer might look something like this: "Hmmm ... I forgot that the history assignment was due today and blew it. I'm going to make sure I get my homework done before I play any more. In fact, I think I'll limit my playing time to Friday and Saturday evenings until the semester is over. My dad dipped into thirty years of savings so that I could have this opportunity. I'm not going to screw up school."

Adults who have these skills tend to function well overall, despite stresses that come up in their lives. They don't hide from problems; they explore ways to solve them. When gaming takes over our self-skills, the ability to function naturally starts to decline. We choose *not* to correct.

We become aware of what's happening *inside* a game and naturally begin to lose our skill at understanding our real bodies. People game all night long and are late for work or school. They skip homework and chores. Some don't bathe regularly, pay their bills on time, or eat meals with their family. They stop spending time with their boyfriends or girlfriends, give up sports or going to the gym. Gaming takes over activities they used to enjoy. They feel moody or unhappy when not gaming. This is functional impairment. Sometimes the impairment starts off as subtle and is gradually built alongside an addiction. Sometimes a person never had the ability to balance his life in the first place.

With some gamers, it can be hard to tell whether they're experiencing impairments. More and more these days, we need computers to live, and people use digital technologies to keep in touch with friends and relatives. While all addicts distort reality so that approaching problems seem far off and convince themselves that real emergencies don't exist, a game's real-feeling rewards can shift our real-life functioning into game functioning. Because games are a type of reality, it doesn't matter that they're illusionary or secondary. Whether it's the adrenaline-pumping action, real people, or a perfect storm of the player and the game — these different in-game goals can help in this process of distortion. They can make it even harder for a gamer to take an honest look at his real life.

Whatever the case, gamers with problems generally don't see what's happening, and when other people try to point it out to them, they get angry and shut them out, and then that annoyance becomes just another reason to play. The people who have to deal with the real-world mess get even angrier, establishing the proverbial vicious cycle. It might look something like this: "I get a rush from playing games, I like the rush so much I don't pause to take care of life. You complain, I get angry at you, I play more to feel better. I do less to take care of life, you get really angry, I get angrier, I play even more to feel better...."

This can play out in different ways, and it's often influenced by wildly different levels of maturity, but most importantly by the differences in self-skills. Adults and children are radically different when it comes to balancing reality and illusion. Children can't function in the same way as adults, because often they're too busy developing more rudimentary skills. In general, however, once someone starts having problems with their basic ability to function, when it's obvious that you or somebody else just can't take care of business, it's probably time to get help. It doesn't matter what we call it: "impaired functioning," "addiction," "problematic gaming," or just "oops," something isn't working.

With so many possible ways of being and acting inside today's games, let alone what's over the horizon, people will continue to enter for a myriad reasons. Gamers without skills at self-awareness often don't understand why they crave games. In many ways they mimic traditional addicts and often ascribe near-magical powers to the addiction. Researchers have shown that these non-game addicts *firmly* believe that they need a substance or behavior to energize themselves, stay psychologically balanced, soothe themselves, become more social or intelligent, sometimes even to experience any pleasure at all. What's more, many also believe that their cravings will never go away, and that not indulging themselves will only make things worse. Chemically, the opposite is almost always true. Feeding the beast will only make it more powerful.

Our resistance to adversity is important, but so are the actual problems that put that resistance to the test. Adversity comes in all shapes and sizes, and very few of us get to decide when and where tragedy strikes. If something painful happens to a gamer in his real, primary world, then games can be a natural choice for coping and recovering. Very often trauma, even if it's just a small helping of it, can be the catalyst for a serious gaming problem.[32] Losing a boyfriend or girlfriend, getting fired, having an acidic fight with your parents, children, husband, or wife. Any of these could become the point where a balanced and healthy gamer takes a turn for the worst. Ironically enough, these catalysts can often be arguments and situations that were slowly introduced by the game itself.[33]

People with co-occurring problems, things like depression, bipolar disorder, or chronic pain, are going to be a lot more receptive to worlds where everything is easy and rewarding.[34] In fact, in almost every major piece of research out there, it's been found that co-occurring problems drastically increase the chances that someone is going to be addicted to something, game or not.[35] It's taken as such a given that some medical professionals don't understand how people can get addicted to games without also having some type of other problem.

Serious co-occurring problems make it all the more important that we understand why a particular person is playing. For example, if a game really is the only place where a teen can feel in control, rewarded, and happy, then simply taking all of that away could be devastating for him. It can also have some shocking consequences for society.[36] This was the case when, in 1999, two teens spent a full year plotting to kill hundreds of their classmates, in the Columbine massacre. In his research into those events, Dr. Jerald Block came to believe that the turning point for these teens was when, on the advice of a therapist, parents simply removed the computer. What they didn't understand was the complexity of the relationships being built between person and computer. In some cases, people can come to enjoy machines as they might a dear friend.[37] Today, in 2008, people can build far more complex relationships with their computers, relationships that aren't always just good or evil.

Whether the problem has been built up little by little, is fueled by functional impairments, starts with a major co-occurring disorder, or some kind of tragedy, some gamers reach the tipping point. This is the phase of an addiction where small steps transform into a sprint, and things truly get out of hand. Nonstop ecstasy is boring. Once a gamer gets used to chemical Nirvana, the game won't be able to give him the old familiar rush. In other words they start to build resistances to some of the chemicals that are being released — namely the dopamine. The more the system is flooded with dopamine, the more it's going to take next time. If a game has topped the to-do list and then elevated itself above the other things that used to be enjoyable, then at some point it's going to be the only reason that the gamer wakes up in the morning.

By now he's already started doing little things in order to play more — cancelling plans to meet with friends, calling in sick to work, and making small excuses. Things have already been slowly pruned from the to-do list, to the point where a gamer is really starting to forget about some of the basic behaviors that he needs to survive. Continuing on this path, even the games won't be enough. Eventually somebody's resistance to the big pleasure buttons being pressed gets too big. He's got to play way too much before the feelings register in his brain.

Unable to meet the brain's demand for stimulation, some players take an honest look at the things they've sacrificed since their gaming got out of whack. They see the difficulties that they currently have in their lives, and they stop, at least until their resistance can die down a bit. Other gamers will go into emergency mode. They will start sacrificing anything that they possibly can to play a little bit more. Remember that a lot of other activities have already been sacrificed by this point. Now a gamer is losing the things which he or she truly needs to survive. Through the eyes of the player, the decision to keep going feels the most logical and natural. After all, playing more is the only thing that's really going to feel worthwhile to the brain; the mediocrity of reality could feel like torture by comparison.

Some gamers do keep playing, and playing, until they hit bottom. Chemically, at this point they've milked the game for every last drop of fulfillment, and their systems simply crash. Functionally, life has stopped working. A gamer has lost his job, his parents no longer support him, there's no money for internet or games, and he's getting hungry. The person may not feel mentally or physically drained; he just isn't getting by any more, not even by manipulating others to take care of him. Emergency mode and hitting bottom are both mentally and physically draining — for the gamer, but also for everyone around him. This is the point where a lot of addicts will pick up the pieces and start to reclaim the parts of their lives that they abandoned in a haze of dragon-slaying. For others, the gaming experience is uniquely possessive.

Sometimes the meanings and relationships that players attach to gaming experiences are enough to keep them playing. Remember that these are physical spaces that look and feel real, especially when they connect us with other living people. Some of what makes these games real can reach out and force a player to sit back down. As with spending time in any other place, players grow fond of the places and used to the people. When their characters are especially powerful, or their gaming skills particularly notorious, players' friends inside these games are usually adamant that they stay. Their absence is felt by the people still playing, and that feeling of being needed can often keep them from leaving.[38] If players can stop and have a moment of clarity, especially when it's clear that they've sacrificed real and necessary things for their secondary lives, then sometimes the denial and haze can lift just long enough.[39] What's unfortunate is that these moments of clarity tend only to come after some form of permanent change.

Gamers can hop out of this cycle at any time, and that can be an extremely rewarding decision. The thrill has gone out of the gaming, and exiting the game leaves someone with dozens of hours each week that they can fill with any number of behaviors. Depending on how badly burnt out a player was on gaming, there's a chance that he'll find at least one of these real things particularly rewarding.

Regardless of the difficulty a gamer has in leaving, coming back to the games, or relapsing, will be easy. It's typical for someone to jump right back into bad gaming, playing just as much as he did at the height of his earlier problems. Whether it's been months or years since he last played, even the most forgetful brain will tend to remember how to reward itself. This is a natural part of making the change.[40] Not every quitting gamer has a serious relapse, but it's a major concern in a society that revolves so completely around entertainment. If your average entertainment junkie doesn't understand how to control himself by the time gaming technologies are commonplace, then he's going to find a fix around every corner. At some point the problem might not be that these technologies are everywhere. What happens when they become a necessity? Once we all *need* these technologies to live our lives, who's ultimately responsible for keeping us safe?

Denial, Blaming and Helping

A lot of people puff out their chests and ask for the simple rule. If we're going to keep our lives balanced and happy, then surely there can be one big rule that tells everyone how much is too much. But answering a question like, "How many hours per day can you play, and still stay safe?" is the tricky part. People lie, to themselves and everyone else. Some will say, "I play 18 hours a day and my functioning is not impaired at all."

Sure, and that's not lipstick on my collar. It's blood. From vampires. Of course my blood is pink and has sparkles in it. Someone playing 18 hours a day is going to have a hard time seeing himself objectively. According to a growing body of literature, humans aren't made to; part of our nature is forgiving transgressions and skewing facts. According to psychology researcher and educator Michael McCullough, "Denial is part of the uneasy bargain we strike to be social creatures."

People who say, "Drinking two beers every day makes you an alcoholic" may have had some experience with drinking, but it's never that simple. There will always be too many differences between individual people to make those kinds of calls. Genetics, tolerance and any number of factors come into play with alcoholism. While two beers don't affect everyone, quite a few more people in this world can get tipsy on just one beer. Two leaves them drunk. If they have children they're responsible for, and that beer has them ignoring (or worse yet abusing) their kids, then this is a *major functional impairment*. People in certain circumstances will be impaired by different things, and everybody has a different set of responsibilities. Where there are dogs, bills, and especially children who need taking care of, playing video games for 18 hours a day most certainly *is* a problem.

We want to make simple rules, like "X hours are okay, but XX hours are not." Humans aren't simple. Each of us enters into the picture with different personalities, bodies, skills, and other characteristics. As a general rule, today's current "general rules" on gaming safely are always guesswork. If you have a well organized life, few responsibilities, no living beings to take care of, and your mom likes doing your laundry, then you can obviously get away with spending *more* time gaming than a person with a job, a twenty-acre yard to mow, six hairy sheepdogs, and two children. All the same, time is a precious enough resource that the individual should be the one choosing when and where he spends it.

Gaming problems aren't just a hive for a few sensational issues. They're unique places, which can pull on psychology and physiology in many ways beyond just addiction or obesity. In some instances they introduce new challenges, even for established areas like functioning. In general, we could say that most adults would have problems maintaining a functional life if they engage in any "recreational" activity, like gaming, watching television, or reading romance novels, more than three hours a day. But such numbers tend to be opinions. That is to say that even if there were research out there to guide such rules, we all live unique lives, online and off.

Realistically, these things really have to be examined on a case-by-case basis. Someone objective has to be taking a look, someone who knows the underlying workings for at least some of the problem. Simple rules are seductive because humans are programmed to think that following one or two hard and fast rules will keep them safe. That's not a wise strategy with video games. Too few people understand enough about the games and the stability of a person to be able to know whether or not they're lying when they brush off problems. Not only do addicts of all shapes and sizes love to deny, to themselves and others, how many hours per day they're playing (that is, if a gamer is even sure of the number to begin with). There might be interesting reasons for gamers to exhibit something beyond denial. Inside the game, other people encourage and acknowledge that way of being. Denial has caused addicts to happily shirk responsibility for centuries, and current human confusion over these online worlds only adds to this.

The worst kind of fair-weather friend for a problem gamer, especially in MMO games, is the one that they meet *inside* a game. Since you're often only as powerful as your in-game friends, not many people in games are going to remind you that sixteen straight hours of playing is probably unhealthy. They're more likely to congratulate you on your progress, then spend more time with your character. Some reward players while they kill themselves, because that player's progression is beneficial to them. Even people who aren't the gamer's friends can prompt them to play more, whether by providing ample competition or leading by example. As more and more people start to invest time in being the baddest and the best, MMO games quickly become a competition to "keep up with the Joneses." Players can either surpass their neighbors, or get left behind.

Practically, most games are set up to be played for long periods of time. It's built into the fabric of the gamer culture, it's encouraged by game marketing, and there aren't enough good stopping points in most games for people to stop, look at the clock, and realize that it's time to sleep. From Bangkok to Berlin, people who play games do seemingly outrageous things once they get their hands on a game that they've been anticipating. They might take a day or two off of work, or turn off their phone for a weekend so that they can play old favorites. This binge culture has been part of gaming culture for quite some time, among many it's an accepted practice. But binging is never healthy. Binge, by its very definition, implies "out-of-control," which is the complete opposite of helpful. It is not, in any way, shape, or form a way to play healthy. What you want is to actually think about how much you're going to play, and

109

conscientiously set aside blocks of time for gaming in a manner that won't harmfully impact your life. Immersion, however, provides an almost blanket invitation for gamers to lose themselves in its pleasurable state change.

Many gamers binge, sometimes without even realizing it. The problem with this is that we aren't self-monitoring while in the throes of a binge. Even spending one whole day on a game can open the floodgates. The more we get used to tuning out our self-monitoring, the more we invite the constant and uncontrolled playing of a binge cycle.

People inside the game world depend on your presence, even pressure you to stay. If a player is surrounded only by other people whose level of play isn't healthy for them, if that's where they do most of their socializing, everyone reinforces how important it is to level and stay focused on the game. Even if *they* can play in a way that's healthy, other players could be having a profoundly negative influence on the people who, beknownst or unbeknownst to themselves, cannot. Across many games, this effect is known as the guild mentality. The entire group gets caught up in the real illusion, and the secondary world goals inside the game world become the fixation of dozens, sometimes hundreds, of real people. Progression takes over, and people inside the group willingly commit themselves to completing ever more demanding goals within the context of the game world. This is the ideal environment to grow a culture of group binging. The focus is on the group's progress, and this sensation can be an acutely powerful draw. Just as normal immersion might be fading for one or two members of the group, here online there's a whole group of people pulling you back in. They need you if they're going to meet these goals, and vice versa.

Group denial is a well-established notion in traditional dependency work. It's powerful in any addiction. Often gamers attempt to sabotage someone who is trying to make healthier choices; talk of "quitting" often threatens their webs of denial. Because other group members don't want to look at their own behavior, there's often a shocking disregard for the individual. When certain people start to quit so that they can take care of the basics, this can prompt intense guilt trips. "You *gotta* be at the raid on Sunday!" or "You're unbelievable! We just gave you the Black Breastplate of Unholy Raging Fireballs! If you take that and leave, then I'll come to your house and kill you!" These comments can have a powerful pull, because so many of the online games require large groups of hugely invested people. Often, as with someone who takes an item and then leaves, the loss can actually hurt the group in very real ways. Most MMO games aren't designed to accommodate power players who want to leave, no matter how sincere their reasoning.

This process isn't uniquely the fault of the gamer or the game. Both play a part. The game designer works hard to make everything in a game easy, straightforward, fun, and satisfying. At the same time, most players and parents today are ill-prepared, in terms of the knowledge and planning that it takes to handle the gaming experience. There has to be accountability with the people who play games, the parents of gaming children, and sometimes even the people around the gamer. Clearly, some can't afford to be as cavalier as they've been in the past. As time passes, video game consumers are going to become aware that getting into a game without first understanding the experience and themselves could be an ignorant move. Parents are especially accountable, because most children haven't even begun to develop the basic skills that allow the balancing of video games. Where in the past society has been somewhat tolerant of parents who dump the kids in front of a television, we're starting to realize that doing the same thing with video games can have harsh and lasting consequences.[41] The same factors that bring on those consequences make video games far more seductive. They can hold a kid's attention much longer.

Addicts, kids or not, don't exist in isolation. Most of them live in some kind of social situation, either with parents, roommates, or a relationship partner. Others are affected by their gaming and affect it in return. As the gamer increasingly loses functioning in real life, others take notice. Problems with basic functioning make life harder for those who live with or love an addict. It makes it *so* hard, in fact, that many of them start having serious problems that develop into their own label: codependent. An addict's behavior is upsetting them so much that they begin to lose their ability to function well in their own lives. They get caught up in trying to control the addict, but don't know how to set boundaries that would be effective, helpful to themselves as well as the addict. One example might be a husband who is so upset that his wife plays all night that he lies awake tossing and turning, unsuccessfully ranting at her to turn off the game. He can't sleep, loses his appetite and doesn't eat breakfast, then misses work the next day — to stay home and argue with her about her gaming habit. Codependency is quite common in gaming situations, whether the addiction is advanced or not.

Emily is a 35-year-old registered nurse who is in the process of divorcing her husband of seven years, Zac. "I haven't felt like his wife for the past three years," she said. "Zac's real wife is his computer, specifically World of Warcraft. He was laid off from his job a year ago, and since then plays almost every hour he's awake. We have a five-year-old son, and I can't even trust him to take Jesse to school. If I work an evening shift, he doesn't bother to stop playing long enough to feed him dinner. Jesse microwaves his own hot dogs."

Emily has found support in an online group for "gamer widows," those whose significant others have emotionally abandoned them for virtual worlds: "I used to beg him to log off and spend time with us, to act like a husband and a dad. Jesse and I would wait for him to finish up what he was doing on the computer before we'd eat dinner — and he'd pay no attention. I complained; sometimes I lost my temper and yelled. I finally realized that I was allowing Zac's addiction to ruin my life, and it's not worth it. Jesse and I deserve better. We're moving on, and I don't think Zac really notices."

The problems being seen by therapists don't just revolve around players. More and more often they're running into one of the many gamer widows, both men and women. The gaming partner often refuses to come in for counseling, however; they find reinforcement inside their virtual network of friends.

On the other side of this coin, real-world *or* online friends who encourage a gamer to engage in a balanced level of social activities can have equal pull in the other direction. Friends, loved ones, and therapists can *enhance* someone's motivation to live a healthier life, but they cannot *create* motivation. An addict gets motivated when he has to feel the pain that comes from seriously failing himself and others. He feels the motivation once the thrill of illusion clears, or is shocked away. When he violates a serious part of his own moral code, crosses a line that he dreads or has a moment where he begins to realize the extent of a problem, then he'll have some chance of doing something about the problem. Motivation can also come from other people, in social interactions that are positive in tone but which force the individual to look at hard realities.

And the online friends are in the best position to do something about this. Should gamers knowingly encourage other gamers to abandon real-world health, wealth, and happiness? Think back to Gary Gygax, the man who helped to start this culture over fifty years ago. The only valid purpose of a game that he saw was entertainment.[42] When gamers turn their heads away from that, it seems that they've lost sight of what it means to be a part of the culture; that's to say nothing about what it means to be a decent human being. When gamers aren't sensitive to the actual people they're playing with, in many ways they deserve for those players to back out, taking powerful gear with them.

Almost anyone who's played in a MMORPG game remembers some kind of "guild drama," especially when someone is trying to quit. Some gamers can step back and say, "But — it's a game!" Many, it seems too many, are willing to bite, claw and drag their ex-friends through the mud if only to keep them doing the dirty jobs a few days longer. There seems a sad dehumanization among some gamers who become locked into the mindset of playing for reward, not playing with people. Certainly this doesn't affect all of them, but rather it seems to explain data suggesting that a significant number report suffering serious effects themselves.[43]

Which begs the question: could or should developers do more to alleviate these problems? Players trust game designers to bring in the fun. It's their job. Game designers can't, won't, and shouldn't make every game more boring. It would be a less than creative solution. At the same time, addiction obviously isn't fun. It doesn't help the player and it doesn't help the people around the player. The industry knows that addiction is bad for business, and for a number of reasons.[44] It alienates potential gamers, repels parents, and keeps gamers on one game rather than buying what's new. At the same time, in this chapter and the last we saw a number of places where the satisfying pieces in a game could be traced back to behavioral psychology, deep-seated human motivations and factors related to traditional addictions. Researchers from some companies have even explained how they would apply some of these to a game in order to make it more satisfying.[45] You can't have those elements and still wonder why you're getting addicts. This stuff isn't rocket science.

Game addictions may not be just the fault of a game or addict, but society tends to expect that the products they buy are safe. If the products aren't safe, then they usually have big eyesore warning labels, instructions for use, or something else that lets the customer know that there's an element of risk. Regardless which side made the biggest contribution, the one constant is that game addiction is always going to be a process, the gamer and the game are always going to work together.

Unfortunately, there's a major roadblock to get past before we can expect game players and game makers to be responsible; we need to get past ignorance. Too few people realize that binge behavior, even our media experiences, can over time rewire the brain in ways that provide specific challenges to balance. The long-term solution here is teaching people how to balance real life with digital life. It isn't fear-mongering rhetoric, nor is it keeping our heads buried in the sand. Professional politicians can get a lot of mileage out of attacking games, and reporters gravitate to the sensational portrayals of gamer fiends neglecting children. On the other side of the fence, most gamers and developers are encouraged to ostracize anyone with a problem as "unstable and psychotic," "inconsiderate jerks," or "giving all of the good players a bad name." Pro-games journalists, even some researchers, seem fixated on portraying the "other side" as slavering anti-games fanatics. Neither approach seems to be helping the people who do have problems. Hundreds of millions of people play games, and countless more are on the threshold of being ushered into the digital living room. This is not a time to bicker; it's a time to understand the power and pull of art.

Five

GAMES ARE
NOT BABYSITTERS

The capacities for maintaining a healthy, balanced life are developed in childhood.[1] In this chapter we're going to look at the basics of what kids need to play right. What might be more important, though, is how gaming during childhood can help or hinder the development of the other important life skills and areas of growth. Sitting down to play a game, even mature adults can get wrapped up in how real-feeling and time-consuming it all is. That's part of what makes games so compelling, but it can also create major disruptions for kids. Video games present a new kind of influence to the growing brain, one that's already had an incalculable impact on society as we know it.[2] As children develop, passing through certain stages, excessive gaming can inhibit the process of growing into a healthy adult. When intense marketing, sex, and violence come along for the ride, not to mention a social space that invites pedophiles and pediatricians alike, can we still even call these games? We know that games can't substitute for a real human being, but do today's games even qualify as "play?"[3]

Kids have needs that they simply can't fulfill through a screen. The younger the child, the more vulnerable they are to missing out on those needs, and so this chapter revolves around how games relate to those needs.[4] Young people need parenting and friendships that bring constant support, nurturing and interaction. They need the right kind of mental and physical stimulation.[5] Children have to learn the basics that underlie the three self-skills of functioning if they want to become healthy, balanced adults.[6] Unrestricted and unguided gaming can keep those abilities at a distance, making them more likely to build all kinds of addictions —

over and above those to games.[7] Young people aren't just growing their brains and bodies; that growth (or lack thereof) dictates their neurological and physical potential later on.[8] Their entire personalities are being shaped. Their future, and consequently *our* future, is on the line.[9]

Grown adults will generally accept that other adults are unique people with different personalities, tastes in food, music, and entertainment. "Sure," we think, "we're all different." At the same time, many people expect all children to be the same. They assume that kids are affected by video games in exactly the same ways, when that couldn't be farther from the truth. Kids all have specific personalities, strengths, weaknesses, and needs. There are too many different things going on for us to make hard and fast rules. Even with only a few years under their belts, two children can be worlds apart.[10] Kids all mature at a different pace. Even though one child, let's say Dana, is fourteen years old, he might not be nearly as well developed in key areas of thinking, emotion, self-control, and judgment as Karen, who is only eleven. Chronological age, or the numbers that we use, doesn't really tell us much about whether a child can handle a certain kind of game. Developmental age tells us whether a child has made progress at *developing* his personality — not just how old he is.[11]

When you think about it, this makes a lot of sense. Saying that a child must be at least thirteen in order to watch this movie doesn't explain *why* a younger kid is going to have problems processing a movie. It's just a rule that we have, and in the end it's a number that doesn't apply to every child. That's why kids who may not have problems understanding some themes can watch these movies when they're accompanied by a parent. That said, your average citizen probably couldn't tell you why their government picked a certain number for drinking, driving, or smoking. To understand the different *whys* of gaming, we're going to have to approach the topic based on how *developmentally* mature a child is. People don't mysteriously grow the parts of their brain that enable psychological maturity just by reaching a certain age.[12]

There's evidence that some games can definitely make things difficult for kids who haven't gotten to certain developmental milestones.[13] This isn't to say that they can't be a part of a balanced diet for a lot of kids. It depends upon how much time a kid is allowed to spend gaming, but also what happens inside the game.[14] Some are going to build creativity and intellect, while others might foster a hunger for excess, violence and consumerism.[15] This tale begins with your shifty and plastic brain.

Your Brain Is Plastic

James is an example of an adolescent gamer who has been left behind by real life. Though he attends high school reluctantly, at age 17 he has very poor grades and no interest in learning to drive a car or get a job. He never thinks about dating. Sports? Outings with friends? *Why?* According to his mother, Teri, James never leaves the virtual world and hasn't since he got his first PlayStation at age six. He often forgets to leave the computer to eat. James was born with a good brain, but it's become lopsided, rigidly molded due to his repetitive and narrow focus on gaming.

Teri is a counselor at a major university and has worked as a substance abuse therapist for 15 years. She sees exactly what's going on, but as a working full-time single mom, she's found it impossible to redirect James. She's been trying for years.

"James has always been an introvert," Teri says, "and I think it was hard on him when his father and I divorced when he was five. He has never been interested in initiating social relationships and he's very strong-willed. He's always had a compulsive drive toward electronic media of any kind, particularly games. When we first got him the PlayStation, I thought it was a cool gift — I saw in just a few weeks he was in trouble with it. Gaming became a way for him to process all his stress and emotions, and he's never been able or willing to discuss things verbally or build friendships with other people.

"It's an ongoing, constant battle," Teri says. "He is indoors all the time, he's online and will never help with chores. If I force him to shut off the computer he will just shut down and sleep. If he's off for very long he starts to have withdrawal symptoms and he becomes hostile and aggressive. He becomes mean. Our relationship has become increasingly negative, and I'm at a total loss about what to do."

Brain plasticity is a term that means the connections made inside our brains can be re-written with enough effort, chiefly if we do the same thing over and over enough times.[16] In children, the brain is *extremely* pliable, which can turn video games into a unique type of hurdle. We might be getting ahead of ourselves, though. There are a few different quirks to how humans' brains and bodies develop, and these nuances have a serious influence on whether children will be able to play video games in a healthy way. Further, they help to illustrate why some adults never learned to.[17]

Today's developmental psychologists have many tools at their disposal. We're going to look at what they're saying about how children are learning and growing in an age of games.

Psychologist and neuropsychological researcher Jane Healy, author of numerous books on child development, says that we need to understand the interplay of nature and nurture. The child's genetics and environment each play their part. Healy says, "Every child inherits a physical brain structure and a timetable for development as well as chemical and electrical response patterns that strongly influence its functioning." So every human inherits a certain structure and a certain way of responding to the world. Each person also has a certain "tempo," meaning that the speeds at which our brains develop tends to be inherited. But we only inherit so much.[18]

Our genes give us a rough outline, but the events of our lives write the actual story. You might say that genes determine our potential. We all have different innate gifts, meaning that there are vast differences among people in physical, intellectual, and artistic abilities. At the same time, these innate capacities are constantly interacting with our *experiences*. We're *always* interacting with our environment, meaning that it's simply impossible to know which is playing the dominant role in our development at any given time.[19]

Psychiatrist Daniel Siegel, an educator and specialist in the care of children and families, is perhaps one of the most well known contemporary voices on the importance of the process of attachment between a primary caregiver and child in the development of the human mind. In his book *The Developing Mind*, Siegel states that relationship experiences have a dominant influence on the young brain, and that healthy attachment is formed when collaborative and contingent communication occurs between a child and her caregiver. Siegel's theoretical model, called "Interpersonal Neurobiology," emphasizes that healthy minds develop through attunement — where parents and children "tune in" to one another's feelings and general mental states from birth on. It's this kind of healthy attachment that leads to the eventual development of a person who naturally has the kind of self-regulation required to keep processes like addiction from occurring. Healthy parents create healthy attachments with their children, in a process that grows healthy brains and healthy minds.[20]

It will further help us understand human development if we look a little at how the brain is structured. To put it very simply, the brain is made up of three parts — the primitive brain stem, the emotional limbic system, and the thinking cortex. The lower parts of the brain develop first, the upper thinking parts of the brain last. In fact, neuroscientists now know that the cortex of the brain is not fully developed until after adolescence.[21] When we say a child is not a miniature adult, we mean that their brains are *entirely* different. They don't think like adults; they don't process emotions like adults; they don't experience the world like adults.[22] Even if they've learned to do a lot of things, like play video games, they still don't have awareness and judgment.[23] A lot of work has to go into supporting a young human while she grows a functional brain and body and develops into a person who can effectively self-regulate.

Thinking does not develop automatically. To paraphrase Jane Healy a bit more, at birth the brain contains hundreds of billions of brain cells, the neurons, but they have to organize themselves. To do the basics, like seeing, thinking, talking, and remembering, these baby neurons build actual, physical connections between one another. For instance, if they repeatedly see and hear two things at the same time, like a dog panting, then their cells will build a connection between those two things. We might call these different pathways synaptic connections.[24] Neuroscientist Joseph LeDoux is famous for his paraphrased quote, "The neurons that fire together, wire together."[25] When we do two things in tandem, especially when we do them a lot, connections can be forged deep within the brain.

Kids arrive in the world with amazing potential to make synaptic connections between different types of neurons. As a child continues to perform certain activities, those connections get stronger and stronger. If other activities are not performed or practiced, those connections don't get formed. Repetition of an experience tends to "set" those neural connections. This process starts at birth and occurs with intensity through-out the childhood and adolescent years. Children are especially vulnera-ble to learning certain habits, and recently we've seen that the brain can form far stronger connections during growth spurts.[26]

But nothing is concrete. We now know that the brain continues to develop — and lose — neural pathways and connections until death. This is what we mean by the term brain plasticity. It's not that your brain is actually made of plastic. Nor is it made of concrete. Things are *always changing* and can be changed *as we grow*.[27] Our synapses arrange them-selves in patterns based upon what we do most. And the brain isn't the only place where we grow. It's connected to a big fleshy lump that occa-sionally needs some attention.

Kids have to use their bodies *and* their brains in order to develop the circuitry to grow up healthy. They develop in an interlocking manner. This process is called sensory integration.[28] Feeling the pull of gravity, learning to move muscles, and understanding the real world's 3-D envi-ronments allow our nervous systems to receive, filter, organize, and make use of the information that we get from the world. Integrating your brain and your body *helps you* to do basic things like walk around, but it also aids other stuff, like emotional stability and your ability to pay attention.[29] While some people obviously have more of this than others, it's not an "on/off" affair. It's not that you either "have" sensory integration or you don't. There's a continuum, and the end result of all of this brain stuff is that we all gain strengths in certain areas.[30]

If we understand these connections between environment and activ-ity, we can see how each brain becomes custom-tailored. Our brains are actually physically shaped by our environments and this includes our inter-actions with others. If we spend our childhood years having lots of witty conversations, the parts of the brain for using language are more fully developed. If we spend substantial time doing physical activities, then we will gain skills in balance, coordination, and body awareness. Repetition of an activity is how both intellectual and physical growth happen; it's how we develop skills and strengths. Lack of stimulation to certain parts of the brain and body may result in intellectual, creative, social, and/or physical deficits.[31]

So, then, what kinds of connections do children need most? It's actually best if they get a variety.[32] Getting a wide array of environmental experiences helps them to develop skills to deal with *all* of the complex challenges that kids are going to face in the big bad world. Kids who don't get that might be lacking in some obvious skills, but the real deficits are often subtle, some of which would be characterized as learning disabilities. Jane Healy says that children with lopsided experiences are likely to end up with lopsided brains.[33]

If we do one activity over and over again, it is likely that we will become really good at it. If that's *all* that we do, then our brains won't get the chance to develop in other areas.[34] And brain development is *integrated* into the body and motor development directly. A brain might be lopsided in the following scenario. Say it's connected to an individual who is intensely skilled at chain healing, long-distance headshots, jumping Mario over tubes or Tetris. When the same person has trouble tying his shoes, you might say that his brain is a bit lopsided.

What's more, physical activity during childhood is critically important to building connections in the brain. Kids need to get on those skates, ride that bike, swing on the swing set, and hang upside down from the monkey bars. They can't just do that stuff through the screen.[35] Physical movement is just as important later on in life. Even once you've grown up, the more that you move your body, the sharper your mind stays. At least 15 percent of American children are now overweight, as are 60 percent of adults. Ten percent are already overweight as toddlers. The bigger we get, the harder it becomes to move, and the more we slow down. Are we justified in worrying that the industrialized world could end up with a generation of sedentary and not-so-smart people?

Spontaneous physical play has diminished dramatically in the past two decades as kids spend more and more time in front of screens.[36] There are now over two million children on drugs for the treatment of ADHD in the U.S.; many speculate that excessive time in front of electronic screens, little physical activity, and limited quality interaction with parents may be a major contributor to the problem.[37] Brains are being trained in new ways that we don't yet fully understand.[38]

Physical sensations are mapped in the brain in very complex ways, and neuroscientists also emphasize a brain function called interoception — your ability to read and interpret sensations arising from within your own body. People who study addictions are also incredibly interested in a part of the brain called the insula.[39] This little piece of brain controls the connection between the brain and the body, and damage to it helped longtime smokers to quit quickly and lastingly.[40] The brain and the body are intimately linked, in ways that we're only just beginning to open up. Being aware of our bodies is an essential piece of functioning. It's the essence of the first two self-skills: awareness and monitoring. When we don't have a basic sense of how the body is doing, we can't know when a behavior just isn't working. We won't be able to see problems forming, let alone do anything about them. A lack of physical experience in the primary world keeps kids from learning to understand their body and mind's basic sensations. It sets the stage for addiction.

Nutrition is also incredibly important for healthy brain/body growth.[41] Kids need sufficient carbs, protein and iron; fruits and vegetables provide building-blocks for brain and body growth. If the game starts to effectively confuse a gamer's stomach, then he could wind up getting too much junk food, even no food at all. In any such case, the brain and body won't be able to build a solid foundation. This is going to have serious consequences for how well he'll be able to think down the line.

Sleep is another key factor. Sleep is essential for taking short-term memories and converting them into long-term memory. Kids also need sleep if they're going to recharge their batteries, essential to being able to tackle the basic problems life throws at a little bugger. Kids who are awake long nights won't develop as effectively as those who get the right amount of sleep.

Overall, it's easy to stay worried when we look at how games could be holding back the brain's natural development, maybe even re-training it altogether. Jane Healy uses the example of a child playing the piano. She takes a sheet of music, turns it into finger movements, and listens to a melody — and she learns to do it all at the same time. Nowadays, computers do a lot more of the combining for us. If that continues, then an entire generation of children might not learn their basic sensory integration.

While experts like Healy are cautious about kids' exposure to technology, at least in its current state, linguist James Paul Gee is enthusiastic about the learning potential of video games. He believes that the very process of having to navigate through the virtual game world stimulates many different kinds of learning. What's more, he believes that we're learning to navigate technology that will be critical to living in a digital society.[42]

According to Gee, "Next to nothing is good or bad for you in and of itself and all by itself."[43] A technology isn't bad just because it's a particular technology. Taken to an extreme, you might argue for or against nuclear fission. It has created bombs the likes of which have wiped out tens of thousands of people in a single stroke and hundreds of thousands more in the days and decades that followed. The same technologies helped to found a power source with utility enough that even now it provides electricity to much of Europe and the rest of the world.

Gee states that television can be good for children, bad for them, or both at the same time. He says that "It's good if people around them are getting them to think and talk about what they are watching, bad when they sit there alone watching passively being baby-sat by the tube." He continues on, saying that it's good when we think about the media that we consume, but that "believing everything you read uncritically is bad for you and for the rest of us, as well, since you may well become a danger to the world."[44]

Gee favors video games which offer the player choices — letting them have control, agency, and the power to choose to solve problems in their own way. It's also helpful if they can see that their decisions have consequences in their world. As Gee puts it, video games can help to develop a child's literacy in "pictures, words, symbols, and graphs." For years, the people studying our education system have talked about how literacy has always focused on understanding only words. But our world is made up of more than words. Anything that helps us to understand the images in our world helps us to understand our world.[45]

What we experience in games can go beyond the textbook. In the right games, we learn problem solving, strategy, reflection, the subtle meanings of different situations, and cooperation. In many games, you simply have to work in groups, and you've got to solve many different kinds of group goals. Many of these skills are lost in some of today's curricula, when, in the U.S. especially, programs like No Child Left Behind literally force certain schools to abandon everything but reading and math.[46]

That said, game learning is not magic; it's fueled by powerful rewards, by dings. Where games most effectively teach, as was mentioned earlier, they do so incidentally. In order to get at specific game rewards, or to express oneself by creating within a game, one must first master the tools. Whether it's browsing gaming websites so as to complete quests and find items, learning the English language so as to better cooperate in-game, or aiming technical skills at improving the computer and game interface, games are effective teachers because those skills are the gatekeepers to uncharacteristically high rewards. Claiming the ability to forge games into a silver bullet of knowledge seems the aim of a corporate alchemist.

As Jane Healy says, "Children still desperately need our human presence: as parents, teachers, loving models and mentors.... The simple fact is that children crave their parents' love and attention far more than anything else."[47] We all start with certain basics, but we're all always learning. When a child is left to wire her brain around illusions, she isn't just missing out on one or two things, like music lessons and swim class. She's failing to diversify her brain in ways that will follow her for the rest of her life. Though the likelihood of an addiction is a part of this puzzle, and it increases dramatically in these cases, addiction is but one challenge to a full life. Since learning to balance games with living takes certain abilities, like the three self-skills, let's look at when those basic building blocks arrive on the scene.

Ages, Stages, Learning and Play

"BludDrinkr will punch you in the face," is the official theme when thirteen-year-old Eric Madden takes his gaming characters online. Blud-Drinkr is notorious in the games he plays. In online shooting games, you had better not call BludDrinkr a newbie. He's been known to wipe out his entire team with grenades, often for fun. In online worlds he does as much as he can to cause grief for other players; he delights in ripping people off when trading and as he lives to brag about it.

"BludDrinkr has no morals. I'll do anything to cause as much trouble in the game as I can," he says with a smile. "The more people who cry about me, the better."

Eric is thin and small for his age, wears thick glasses, and is known around school as the quiet dorky kid. He attends church with his parents every weekend, is liked by his teachers, and is generally polite to other kids in school. His parents brought him to therapy as his grades have dropped from As and Bs to Ds and Fs in the past year, and he spends all his free time gaming. Eric's parents are highly conservative and religious. They don't know anything about the games he plays or the personas he takes on.

"Gaming is the only meaningful thing in my life," Eric told Shavaun on his first visit. Describing what the gaming experience is like for him, he lights up, smiles, raises his voice, and becomes animated. It's like flipping a light switch — all of a sudden emotion and color rush to his face. BludDrinkr can express feelings that good guy Eric can't, and he sees the gaming world as a great place to do it.

"I don't really know why I turn into someone else in the games," he says, embarrassed. "I'm a really nice person in real life. I never treat anyone bad, I never curse. I know when I play I'm a total asshole."

Eric doesn't understand what he's doing or why he's doing it. As much as Eric and BludDrinkr could appear to be multiple personalities, Eric is using his online persona to express those feelings he has been taught are unacceptable to feel in real life. He's been taught that "niceness" is important above all else and that anger is never appropriate. Instead of finding productive solutions to his real-world problems, Eric uses gaming as the one strategy he has to tolerate life. Having to be "nice" all the time is a burden, especially when he doesn't have the self-awareness to even know how he feels most of the time. In real life Eric is a nice guy with no power. In the game, however, BludDrinkr is on a very short fuse.

Developmental psychologist David Elkind has noted, "Screens are not going to go away. The challenge is to find the right balance between screen play and real play."[48] Kids develop based on their brains *and* their experiences, but basic things have to happen before they can play like responsible adults. Depending on their developmental age, they could be having game experiences for vastly different reasons. As they graduate to different developmental milestones, there are unique places where gaming can go wrong. While the following gives age ranges for the different stages of childhood, bear in mind that there aren't hard and fast rules.

During infancy, toddlerhood, and the preschool years, roughly from birth until age four, children are growing brains in ways that allow them to become aware of themselves as human beings.[49] They're learning to understand and control their bodies. They think concretely and learn experientially. We're talking the basic basics, like the perils of gravity. By emotionally bonding with and learning to trust caregivers, they're building the *fundamental* foundations of emotional development. Learning through their sensory systems, like eyes, ears, and touch, is *critical*.[50] Kids need lots of physical contact, movement, and the opportunity to explore the world with their bodies. They initially communicate by crying, a period of glee for parents everywhere. Later, they gradually progress through phases of rudimentary language development. They are driven to manipulate objects around them, stacking things, dropping things, pushing over vases, and tasting what the cat made.

All this activity is categorized as *play*. It's unstructured, spontaneous, and driven by the child's need to learn. As trendsetting Italian educator Maria Montessori said, "Play is the child's work."[51]

During their early years kids are not able to play *with* other children. They don't have skills for interaction and aren't aware that the other person has needs and feelings too. Jarod hits Justin over the head when he wants the toys Justin has been playing with. Jarod screams and bites Justin. This is entirely normal. Social play doesn't develop until the upper preschool years. Around that time kids begin to develop the awareness (through synapses and neural pathways) that allows them to play cooperatively with other kids.

Morally, young kids see themselves as the center of the world. They don't have an internal sense of right or wrong. If they did, then they wouldn't make noise during an opening night showing of anticipated movies like *A Knight's Tale*. What they do learn is that certain behaviors — like hitting baby sister — will result in punishment. During these years kids learn primarily by physical exploration of their world and through imitation of those around them. In short, kids learn through play.

Good preschool education, either at home or in a formal setting, should allow a wide array of toys for manipulation that allow for the natural development of skills that are necessary precursors for the development of reading, math, and getting along with others.[52] Young kids aren't capable of sitting still for long periods of time, if at all, and don't learn by formal instruction or university lectures. The early years of life are not when kids should be passively sedentary, for *any* substantial length of time, in front of *any* electronic media.[53] The American Medical Association has made a serious recommendation that children not be in front of *any* screen before age two. Being parked alone in front of a television may occupy them briefly, but it's not really helping their brains to grow. Remember, that they most need stimulation during growth spurts, and this time is loaded with them. An hour or so spent sitting on a parent's lap while a game or movie is shared is not likely to be detrimental — as long as the parent is paying attention to their needs for interaction and the content of the program is not visceral or graphic.

One of the greatest dangers during this stage involves parents who are gaming and ignoring their kids' needs. Parental warmth and emotional responsiveness are needed for the eventual development of our self-awareness and self-monitoring abilities. Without these, the child will grow into an adult who simply doesn't understand themselves or how much they play.

During the early elementary years, from ages five or six through nine or ten, kids take play to a slightly higher level.[54] They hone skills in reading, writing, keyboarding, and math, and their play is often self-initiated and richly imaginative. They create their own stories and imaginary worlds in role-plays, through art, and the use of more sophisticated toys. They learn the rules of social behavior and how to play cooperatively with others, realizing gradually that other people have feelings that are important too. They are capable of developing the ability to groom themselves, bathe, and brush their teeth — though they may need regular reminders. They're also learning to fine-tune their motor control, their ability to walk, run, and generally cartwheel around.

Kids at this age think concretely and can't really imagine future consequences.[55] Little Courtney does not realize all sugar and no toothbrush could have an adverse affect on her dental health. She just doesn't have the ability to imagine the future. Derrick does not realize that his problem with escaping intestinal gas may produce sounds and odors that will bother others.

Kids' physical coordination improves as they learn things like tying their shoes, riding a bike, drawing, or playing volleyball. While this sensory integration is a crucial first step for a kid's development, none of it would happen effectively without the encouragement and support of caregivers, or without regular opportunities to engage in plenty of different activities.

In the upper elementary years, friendships, achievement in school, and some form of athletic activity become important, because these things create the foundation necessary for mastering certain key events later on in life.[56] If children can't get at least some happy exposure to making friends, making grades, and staying active, things later on will only become more difficult and less rewarding.

This motivation to learn, grow, and succeed is fed by achievement.[57] Success feeds further success, and leads to trying new things, taking new risks, and ultimately mastering new skills. Kids need time to try out lots of activities and wear a variety of different hats — all to see what best fits their interests and abilities. The child who has built up a sense of competency at ages 8, 9, and 10 has a greater chance of feeling confident as an adolescent.

But kids aren't stupid. Research has shown that they know when they're getting empty praise.[58] When a child gets congratulated whether or not the work was bad, they then feel less encouraged to do more. Alternatively, when they've done good work, and they get the same praise as somebody who didn't, they become equally incredulous. What they need is *specific* praise, actual feedback based on what they've actually done well. They could find plenty of rewarding feedback in a game — but if that game is only a single non-educational activity, then that might actually distract more than help. While success drives success, some failure in life is inevitable. This is why it's so important that young kids experience as many different things as possible. With all the differences between children, there's no telling what they'll truly love, or find intrinsically rewarding. One behavior shouldn't block out everything else. Just imagine an adult who loses confidence in the only part of themselves that they themselves admired. What has she got left?

It's important for everyone to understand their own emotions and motivations. Kids are capable of learning a lot about their emotions at this age if parents themselves are emotionally intelligent and use vocabulary that includes feeling words.[59] Parents should talk about both their own feelings and needs and feelings and needs of others and help a child identify her own. This helps kids develop empathy, moral thought, and once again, builds skills for self-awareness and self-monitoring.

This is a time when video games may be introduced into a child's life, as they are able to start thinking strategically. The key here is to make sure that games don't dominate other brain-building activities. Games are made to be inherently fun, welcoming and rewarding. If a child is having a hard time developing in other areas, or if there are serious environmental or genetic impediments, these kids are going to be far more prone to getting accomplished in a game and few other areas. If kids can balance reality and games, and then find video games that develop thinking skills, creativity, and cooperation with others, then all the better. There are no real hard and fast rules for how much time in front of the screen is too much. It depends upon the child's maturity, personality, and needs, but in general, more than one to two hours a day could be risky. The American Medical Association actually recommends that kids have no more than one to two hours a day of "screen time," time spent in front of television *or* computer screens.

In their report, they state, "The Council on Science and Public Health recommends that ... our American Medical Association, in accordance with the position of the American Academy of Pediatrics, support the recommendation of 1 to 2 hours of total daily screen time, and that the total time allotted to playing video games should be included in that 1 to 2 hour allotment." What's more, it makes a world of difference when parents sit down to play alongside their kids.

Kids at this age should not be playing online. This is something we'll come back to, but they just aren't capable of making sense of the kind of socially negative behavior and sexualized images and activity commonly exhibited by others in MMOs. Remember, they learn by example and don't yet have the ability to analyze or think critically.

Adolescence, or around ages 12 to 18, is one of the toughest phases of life, so much so that it's been branded "the terrible teen years."[60] Life gets harder. At the same time, an adolescent's success largely depends on whether he felt accomplished in different developmental tasks of the earlier years. Many kids have not had the environmental support they need to do well during this time, and nothing seems to come easy for them. Since success feeds motivation, kids who have not experienced social and academic success during earlier years are apt to withdraw, lack motivation, or engage in anti-social behavior.

And then there's puberty. It hits everyone at different times, and this rattles everyone's identity. Kids are very self-conscious about being "different" from their peers, they can start to see themselves in a harsh light, and most assume everyone else is observing them they same way. And since puberty hits them all with all the force of a hormonal A-bomb, most also become preoccupied with sex and being sexually attractive; everyone wants to be considered "hot."

And we all remember how much fun classes and schoolrooms were. These days, there are intense pressures to succeed academically, but not everyone has had a chance to develop all the skills needed to get through school. As kids age, academic life gets progressively harder, increasingly more stressful, and more complicated. At the same time, many kids have not grown their minds in ways that allow them to learn what's expected. Without ample developmental maturity, chances are slim to none that they'll be able to handle it all and make good choices.[61]

Parents tend to demand a lot from kids, not realizing how stressful this time is or what their internal struggles may be. Kids stop talking to their parents. They withdraw and become private. Yes, it's completely normal. No, it's not fun for anybody, but it's part of the natural process of wanting to break away and establish one's own identity. Households become tense, sometimes miserable. Teens no longer want to hang out with the family, and they resent doing chores around the house. They engage in power struggles with parents, teachers and each other. Kids get hostile and parents get reactive, and everyone may get depressed and anxious. What great fun!

If earlier phases of development have not gone well, it becomes very apparent during the teen years.[62] If kids are supposed to be earning good grades in school, dating the hot guy or girl, getting a job and managing money, yet they can't, it's no wonder this is a time when kids are at special risk for compulsive gaming. Not only do you get to escape the big bad world, but you're dropping yourself into worlds designed to make you feel successful.

Unrestricted access to MMO worlds, without any parental involvement or understanding, can be a very bad thing. These games connect a number of people, many of whom assume that young children do not play, and so they will discuss topics ranging from rape to racial hatred in a way that can be candid and outrageous, though very often facetious. Facetious as it may be, younger kids will not understand. It isn't hard to see why some parents forbid online games, even for kids as old as 16 or 17.

On the other side of the coin, it's easy to see why kids of all ages want to play. Someone who feels like a loser in his or her primary life can become a hero or a sexy babe in a secondary life. Games are designed to be satisfying, and they satisfy in many different ways. You just have to pick an experience that appeals to you, and before you know it that experience could be the most, if not the only, appealing thing you've got. All it takes is enough time in the game to train the brain. While a little success is probably great for these kids, and they all develop complex relationships with the worlds themselves, too much play will almost inevitably come at a cost to developing crucial other skills. We live in a complicated world, and it can be painfully obvious when a game has kept a kid from learning how to live in it.

While the screen may show children make-believe images, they are having real experiences. One shouldn't forget that all human experience is real, on some level. Even dreams affect us; the land of nod has long been able to influence the decisions humans make and paths that they take. Games take this farther when they make high-stakes wins and losses that don't disappear once you turn off the game. Games are a very real experience, and it's not the least bit uncommon for people, adults and children alike, to venture into games so as to live out a psychologically meaningful aspect of their lives.

Think back to Eric Madden, or BludDrinkr. He felt weak and powerless in all of his real-life situations, then used the game as a way of transforming himself. He took on gruesome names, built himself up as chaotic and violent, yet was living in a virtual persona divorced from his character in reality.

In a nutshell, he says, "I'm not sure why I do it." That's a critical point in understanding why people get into problems with addiction. People often don't understand their drives, why they do what they do.

It's important that kids grow up learning about emotions and how to handle them. They learn this from living with parents who are warm, involved, emotionally aware, and who engage in non-judgmental conversation with them. With the right kind of support, they become "emotionally intelligent." They deepen their understanding of what they're feeling at any given time, which gives them the ability to regulate themselves once they realize that things are going downhill. These aren't new concepts; they're the skills of self-monitoring, self-awareness and self-correction that adults use to stave off addiction.[63] If they don't develop the foundations to those skills in childhood, then they may never develop them.

Sex Sells

"I honestly didn't expect my parents to notice," says fourteen-year-old Caitlin Johnson. "I thought it would all work itself out."

She doesn't know why she went online and used her mom's credit card to buy $9,000 in "luxury teen items," though her parents had some pretty clear ideas. When her mother rushed to make an appointment for a clinical diagnosis, she expected Caitlin to need psychiatric medication and long-term therapy. She bluntly asked, "Could this spending be a symptom of bipolar disorder or some kind of psychotic behavior?"

Caitlin is shy, with long dark hair, large eyes, and a face that anyone would find pretty. She's a straight–A student and had never been in nine thousand dollars' worth of trouble before. Her parents had allowed her to hold onto an extra credit card "just for emergencies" while they left her with relatives for a few days. Caitlin's interpretation of "emergency," included the need for $300 pairs of jeans, designer party dresses, and name-brand perfume — *lots* of perfume.

"Maybe it's my nose," she says, "It's bigger than a regular person's nose. And I'd like to be as tall as a model — at least 5'10"."

Like a lot of girls at this age, Caitlin gets thrown into a state of panic at her appearance. She spends hours studying herself in the mirror and worrying about nonexistent flaws. She plows through stacks of teen fashion magazines when her parents think she's studying — and she's on her laptop browsing online shopping websites into the wee hours of the night.

Caitlin isn't psychotic or bipolar. Her "mental illness" developed out of being a normal kid plopped headlong into an industry that knows how to profit from girls like Caitlin. Worrying is a trademark of adolescence. In Caitlin's case, these anxieties and perceptions were amplified by the constant influx of television, magazines, and online messages. She wants to look like the supermodels she dotes on; without guidance that can work out a solution based on her, she'll have a hard time resisting advertisements that promise to grant wishes — wishes they seeded. People growing up with credit cards and unmonitored internet access are going to have an easy time getting a little carried away. That is, if you think that $9,000 is only a little.

Caitlin was asked, "Were you worried about what your parents would do when they got the bill?"

She replied, "I just didn't think that far ahead."

According to the Census Bureau, there are currently 25.2 million teens aged 13–18, and in the United States their purchasing power is substantial. If you add part-time job earnings, allowance and the average amount of their parent's money they spend every year, teens compose a $195 billion market. Over a third of teens hold part-time jobs, working 18 hours a week, on average, and earning $483 per month. They're using their disposable income first and foremost for clothes, followed by eating out, cars, movies, and cell phones. A whole class of industry is catering to them like never before.

Many marketing firms and corporations, some explicitly, treat children and adolescents as a niche consumer market to be exploited, with no concern for their development. A lot of us think it, some talk about it, but very few of us actually take an active interest in whether kids can be hurt by marketing buzzwords like "branding," or "leveraging." These words might seem innocuous at first, but think about it. If you have children, or plan on having them, would you like your children to be "leveraged?" Would *you* like to be "leveraged?" The bottom line is that consumerism is king.

If it really has gone too far inside video games, then what does that say about the real world? Eight-year-olds have laptops, broadband, and iPods. Clothing makers market kiddie-sized thong underwear. Young teen girls on MySpace imitate the sometimes pornographic advertising images they see, trying to out-sex each other by posting revealing, "hot" photos. Some are younger than thirteen or fourteen. Pedophiles have noticed. We all choose different ways to make ourselves sexually attractive, but how young is *too* young? The more we learn about child development, the more certain it seems that kids *are* being harmed by the "pressure" from marketing. Because media images and messages hit kids who haven't fully developed, many are copying behavior that they see around them with no concept of what they are doing, why they're doing it, or the long-term consequences. They've been given tools that facilitate adult behavior without the brain to understand what they're doing.

According to a 2006 survey done by a marketing research firm, the Harrison Group, adolescents aged 13–18 in the U.S. spend over 72 hours a week connected to media (internet, cell phone, television, music and video games). The average teen instant-messages with 35 people at least three hours per week. High-schoolers instant-message friends in the midst of their classes and then post details of every drama in their blogs. While blogging allows for all kinds of connections that were, even four or five years ago, difficult to make, some kids come to therapy traumatized over what other kids have posted about them on *MySpace*. Some have killed themselves. This communication is real. It isn't just a story that a child has an experience of.

At least 68 percent of teens have created blogs, which allows for a large and immediate forum for adolescent drama. Many kids report problems with online bullying. Parents, for the most part, have no idea what's going on. Most wouldn't even know where to start.

It's normal for kids to be peer-oriented during their teens and to desire distance from their parents. They never want their parents to know everything they're up to — that's part of the psychological maturation process.[64] At the same time, what's happening online is unprecedented. The sheer number of technological tools that kids have at their disposal influences every aspect of their lives and relationships. Going back to the beginning of this book, these kids now have fully functional secondary worlds at their disposal. These worlds fly under the radar of kids' parents, but also often of law enforcement and the authority that kids need in order to be healthy. Ironically enough, kids may jump into these sexy and rebellious secret lives from the comfort of their own bedrooms.

Drop the Kids Off at the Deathmatch

Games are special because they can very effectively draw people into worlds. It's usually just fine, because a functional adult is going to have the tools she needs to separate that fantasy from reality. She's going to be able to step back into the real world once she's done. Too bad kids don't have that kind of self-awareness. They're busy learning about the real world, making connections, being imaginative, and building basic thinking skills. And because a lot of what they're getting is the basics, some are going to take things pretty literally.

A young kid with unrestricted access to a computer will make connections based on what he sees. Many parents blindly fall into thinking that their child is reading about Martin Luther King, Mahatma Gandhi, and the scripture of their family's religion, when they have never actually taken the time to look. The internet houses information on many good topics, but also plays host to sexual predators and free and intensely gory video games, and is frequently referenced by pop culture for its never-ending stores of pornography.

We can say with surety that violent behavior never results from a single cause. Rather it results from a combination of risk factors which include inherited tendencies, or nature, versus things like childhood trauma and the quality of home life, or nurture (or a lack thereof). This makes every kid different, processing real violence and violent media in unique ways. While these factors are different for everyone, there are some basic problems that should signal violent media as something to avoid.

What this means in English is that being "exposed" to video gaming isn't a silver bullet. Certain media are not going to automatically cause all children to become deranged and violent killers. Rather, what this does mean is that every child is *different*, that some kids are at more risk for committing violence than other kids are. While some kids can play violent video games without losing the ability to contain feelings of aggression, which research has shown *may* be stimulated, some kids will not have that level of control.

Once again, we have to be tuned in to the differences and needs among children. If somebody is responsible for parenting a child and that child has certain risk factors, then that parent should probably take violent games out of the equation. Yet just tugging them away, without first understanding play, can be disastrous.

Columbine remains one of the most gruesome school shootings in American history, and it could have been far more devastating. It has been estimated that the propane bombs placed inside the school cafeteria could have killed an added 448 people. It is also unique in being one of the first shootings to have been largely linked to video games.

When something like this happens, we often blame specific things. According to Dr. Jerald Block, M.D., in his analysis of the shootings, some of the things we blame are bad parenting, a traumatic childhood, psychosis, bullying, peer pressure, or the idea that it's a copycat killing. But Block doesn't find that any of these are significant enough to have prompted the year of planning, premeditation, and bomb-making that went into the attack.

In fact, one of the most striking features to these two is how normal they seemed. They enjoyed movies that many readers of this book may consider classics: *The 5th Element, Aliens, The Rock, Predator,* and *Natural Born Killers.* They played many of the most popular games of the time: X-Com, Command and Conquer, Quake, Diablo, and Warcraft (the predecessor to the MMO World of Warcraft — currently played by over eleven million people). While it's uncertain from their scribbling whether they love or hate the following, they make references to *Mystery Science Theatre 3000* and WWF's Mick Foley (known as Mankind in 1999). The normalcy of these killers is perhaps one of the most compelling and staggering aspects to Columbine.

These two teens were highly complex and intelligent, and they had very complex reasons for playing games. The approach taken by psychiatrists and parents involved treating games as a cancer to be cut out, rather than an avenue for having a range of meaningful experiences. Dr. Jerald Block suggests that the Columbine shooters may have only began planning their famed siege on their school *after* games were removed by parents, which happened on the advice of a therapist.

Yanking away games, once someone has started to play badly, may have consequences not unlike flushing away a drug addict's junk. There will be withdrawal symptoms that can be volatile, and you don't know in advance exactly what you're going to get. Every individual is going to start playing for individual reasons. While there can certainly be negative consequences to play, games can also play a major self-medicating role for people with serious problems.

When someone has developed any type of dependency on gaming, he is often dependent upon playing just to maintain a state of feeling "normal." Just like a drug addict, he will have serious mood and behavior reactions if that game is taken away without a planned withdrawal program. Some people become depressed, some angry, many become both. They may have been using gaming to mask feelings that are very powerful; if those emotions come to the surface suddenly — and the gamer has no skills to cope with them — it can be overwhelming.

Block doesn't see that any of the traditional explanations for youth violence come into play at Columbine, but rather that something unique may have happened in the case of Klebold and Harris. It has to do with how they learned to relate to the media. They were deeply immersed in modifying (commonly called "modding") and changing their own areas inside the game Doom, and they prided themselves on their gaming abilities. These were all different areas where they felt successful — accomplished. It's reported that ID, the creator of their favorite game Doom, actually made changes to sequels according to suggestions of these two killers. Nobody, not even the therapists working with them, seemed to consider that this was relevant.

There's enough money in the games industry these days that if parents were to discover that their children were creating 3-D game environments, they might very likely be pleased. Even if the images created were disturbing, there's something significant about the psychology of creating worlds. It's a recipe for disaster when therapists and parents don't consider the experiences being had and the real effort being put forth. If therapists and parents understood then what they might now about these technologies, could we have stopped this?

Two young people who seemed to want to be caught, seemed to blunder in the hopes of having their plans discovered — appeared to begrudgingly go through with their plans to destroy a school. As Block rightly points out, we'll never truly know exactly what was going through the minds of the killers. Even if they were alive today, there's no telling how much we would be able to extract. What we *can* understand is that calling something "virtual" doesn't mean that it's any less real.

The Right to Play

"The right to play belongs to everyone." — Kofi Annan, then Secretary-General to the United Nations

Kids need play to grow up into healthy adults.[65] Two-year-olds play with blocks. Ten-year-olds play baseball. Kids and their parents play MMO games like Second Life or World of Warcraft. Eighty-year-olds play brain games on their handheld Nintendos. Everybody seems to be *playing*, but is every kind of play the same? When two six-year-olds spend an entire Saturday playing in the back yard, is that really the same as spending the same amount of time playing in a virtual world? While it seems obvious that video games aren't always the same as traditional play and that some games definitely aren't for younger kids, can video games give kids the essential play that they need to grow?

Children's play, even in the very recent past, usually meant some kind of physical play, actively exploring the world with the body and the senses. Kids don't need to be directed on *how* to play; in a supportive environment, they imaginatively turn anything into a toy. They create stories in their heads; cardboard boxes become castles and sticks become horses. Play in early childhood is critically important and should never be looked at as a waste of time. This is the process which allows an infant to gradually develop into an adult, and it's what educator Maria Montessori ultimately meant when she said "Play is the child's work." This is why the United Nations has declared that play is *an essential human right*. But what about video games? Are they the same play that's being defended by many of the world's most influential minds?

David Elkind believes that "screen play" has completely different qualities from "real play." Besides the obvious fact that you're not moving around much when you're sitting at the computer, why isn't "screen play" really the same thing as "real play?" According to Elkind, kids are losing out on self-generated play.[66] When a kid says to herself, "This stick is a pony," the stick becomes a pony and she plays around with it. When kids have an unstructured environment, then they naturally and spontaneously play.

Unstructured and spontaneous self-generated play, letting our imaginations run wild, is what grows our bodies and integrates them with our thinking.[67] The static and unchanging environments in most games just don't provide that. The games present children with imagery that they can't change in the same way that they change their world during make-believe. When children see the video game's chicken, it's just a chicken. In reality the chicken can be transformed into a troll—all in the mind of a child. Elkind, among others, sees this shift as something that could add to poor health and damaged intellectual and social-emotional development. Kids, he says, simply need unstructured and spontaneous play to grow up to be healthy people.

In real life, our imaginations start by turning sticks into ponies, and this is really just the staging ground for even more imagination. Little girls will have tea parties, play house or maraud the high seas as pirates. Young guys will play with snap-together building blocks, pretend to be comic-book action figures, and will sometimes also get suckered into playing house. Eventually girls and boys play video games. While these can take us into stories with more depth, we'll have a very hard time understanding the game, or playing healthy, without first being able to flex our imagination muscles. Self-directed play happens without rules, without limitations, and in the real world. It helps us to develop our ability to reason and to be able to later perceive the difference between reality and fiction.

But we also cannot gloss over how sedentary today's games are and the long hours that some gamers sit. Many games fail at giving kids the physical activity that's necessary to develop sensory integration. If kids only ever sit down for their play, then they aren't going to learn the basics of receiving and making sense of their surroundings. They'll learn to operate inside worlds that require key clicks for walking, and not the one where we've got highly developed muscles for walking. If kids sit too much, then they're not getting the bare minimum of physical activity for their brains to work right.

But games are changing, especially when it comes to how much players get to be creative and how much they get to move around. For now the games that we have don't make it easy for us to create whatever we want. They could.

Dr. Richard Bartle, co-creator of the first virtual world, recently spoke about imagination and creation. When he first started programming worlds, he had to know the intimate workings of bulky and clunky 1970's computers. He had to understand electrical engineering, had to be able to program in *and* modify old computer programming languages, and essentially had to then create an entire back-end for an entire world. Then, and only then, those worlds could be colored with "a little bit of imagination on the top." Looking to the future, he believes that within the next ten or fifteen years we'll all be building our own online worlds as a matter of course. Bartle says, "The less technology that people need to know, the more people will build virtual worlds.... You don't need to know how your internal combustion engine works in order to drive a car."[68]

Even now, players are starting to break away from the image of the sedentary gamer, toiling over their games in a chair. Games like Dance Dance Revolution (DDR) and many on the Nintendo Wii can get people off of their respective backsides and can get them flexing their arms and their legs. DDR gives players a mat, and the game requires that they "dance" along to the music provided. The Wii has a controller that can simulate boxing, tennis, and the swinging of a sword.

And while future games may keep us moving, or put us into the place of being able to create the deepest desires of our hearts, games are collections of rules. Imaginative and spontaneous play, especially the kinds that we find in very young children, the kinds that they need to start with, have no rules. The real-world stick could be a pony, or it could be anything of their choosing.

While games might be able to do some things, and in time they'll be able to do them in impressive ways, they will never be able to replace the play that happens in the primary world. For now, we don't have a great climate for groundbreaking and creative games. These visual environments are too well suited to getting adrenaline running. It's too tempting for big entertainment companies to make immersive war zones. They make more money with them. Games aren't being built to support young kids, or even to take adults into groundbreaking experiences. Right now the vast majority of video games showcase violence, gore, sex, and irresponsibly immature drama. Just like television. The ones that do create stories tend to do so in an environment that more revolves around heart-quickening action.

Games are not babysitters. Parents may be more overworked and underpaid than any time in recent memory, but that's hardly a legitimate excuse to leave the children, unsupervised, with games. If you are a parent, or may ever become one, then play the video games your child plays, and watch the shows that they watch. The media is giving them real experiences. However real or fake the story may be, our experiences of them are always real, and there are some things that no child should ever have to experience.

Six

THE ROAD AHEAD

Each previous chapter has had the job of bringing together bits of knowledge which deal with the problems and pathologies in gaming, especially gaming to the point of "addiction," or dependency. In so doing the chapters have worked to answer a lot of "How?" questions. How is it that games have grown so quickly? How do they grapple the imaginations, attention, minds, and bodies of human beings? How do they addict? How do children fare?

Some of the people we brought in were relatively old. Socrates, J.R.R. Tolkien, Marshall McLuhan, some had been looking at the effect of media on our minds since specific media were young. Many of the people brought in have ideas that are newer and fresher. From people like Norman Doidge and Jane Healy to Nick Yee and Florence Chee, they apply a perspective to media experiences that helps our thinking to become more crisp. Having brought these ideas together, it seems possible that games provide draws that are rarely discussed without too much sensationalism or too little real information.

Addiction, though it's worked as our sherpa, our guide through some problems and possibilities in secondary worlds, isn't the only issue that should give us pause. Having explored how addiction is fueled by immersion, player motivations, and child development, among other things, it's important to mix these together. From this vantage point, it may be possible to draw larger themes from the research. This chapter points to some of the related questions on the effect games might have on individuals, society and our world.

Crossing the Line

We see a children's playground. Next to a slide and brightly colored playground toys, little girls and boys sit in the sand. An older man approaches one of the young girls. He says, "Wanna cuddle some? May I kiss you?—You decide where. My little, sweet girl." This is the pixelated scene filmed, narrated and aired by German show *Report Mainz*, following reports of "ageplay" in the game Second Life. Ageplay is the name given a practice where two digital avatars, at least one made to look very young, engage in different types of intercourse. The phrase "ageplay" is telling. To call any molestation "play," whether real or imagined, is typical of the cognitive distortions used by sex offenders. The BBC reports, "Whilst in the U.S. 'virtual' child pornography is not a crime, in Germany it is punishable by up to five years in prison."[1]

They also mentioned that the German investigative reporter behind the program had been invited to attend virtual child pornography meetings for about $3 U.S. The same people then put him in touch with traders of actual child pornography.

The German report goes on to show images, the genitals edited out, of a bald man seeming to have sex with a child, then an older man with a beard. There are children tied down to wooden devices. The report then shows a children's bedroom; there's a girl with a white dress and bow. A voice says that some Second Life residents will have relations with over a hundred child avatars in succession.

One of *Report Mainz*'s guests, Lutz Ulrich Besser, notes that this lowers a pedophile's inhibitions within the game *and* real life. All forensic specialists would agree. "These patterns can define later actions, thus enabling them later to find victims more easily. This is like a playful preparation to be a victim and a playful preparation to be a criminal."

In this German interview and throughout the internet, Linden Labs, the publisher of Second Life, takes an aggressive stance against the real child pornography. That said, it's been unclear whether Linden Labs' attacks against ageplay, the simulated flirting, voyeurism, sex, and sexual torture involving young-looking avatars, were simply for appearances. To understand why a company, let alone a community of "residents" (the term "players" seems inapplicable here), would be against blanket regulations distinguishing between appropriate and harmful actions ("play," too, seems the wrong word), one has to understand what some of these worlds provide: volition. A surreal level of personal choice, a heightened level of volition that can fly in the face of accepted mores, whether in the primary or the secondary world.

This is partly to do with the chimera of media experience, the "realness" of the texture juxtaposed with how much it empowers the mind. In games like Second Life, that texture certainly exists, yet stepping into that world does more than remove the constraints of the physical body. In some of these secondary worlds people can effect major change on the environment. They can shape their bodies and mold whole landscapes, all to personal tastes. Moreover, in the internet's quest for personal freedom, residents of many secondary worlds and online communities are encouraged to pursue any transitory thought, no matter how unusual. This has sparked the eruption of whole cultures of people who act, react, dress, and are shaped in impossible ways. Some suggest that it has allowed people with uncommon fetishes to group in ways impossible in the real world.

The Gorean, for example, are one of the most apparent of these unique cultures to emerge in places like *Second Life*. Based off of a series of novels which take place on a planet populated by stolen humans, mostly women stolen as slaves, Goreans espouse a philosophy of dominant men and servile women. Their clothing in secondary worlds tends to reflect this, often portraying men in an almost heroic stature, where women are often near-nude, sometimes in chains or in torture situations. Many find any enactment of abuse unacceptable, whether the behavior involves slaves or children.

With these forms of so-called "play," grave boundaries can be pressed. In most every country in the world, there are lifelong consequences to even representing the behavior, let alone pursuing it. The almost complete majority of the world sees it as unforgivable, a black mark that follows a person. The line between healthy and not in these worlds is between fantasy and actuality.

The problem is that for those interested in children, the fantasy is a powerful actuality. Recognizing the process of brain plasticity — how repeated actions develop and strengthen neural pathways which lead to new behavior — paints this "fantasy" in a damning light.

Others suggest that these places are purely based in make-believe and that each individual's right to volition must be respected. Even if one takes that stance, we all have to admit that there is no way of monitoring the ages of the persons behind the avatars and whether or not they have a history of abusing others sexually and/or violently. There's no way to know who is crossing the line.

Individuals in such secondary worlds, the "games" more focused on creative production and social processes, may not yet be exposed to the same reward structures which pull in gamers in commercial secondary worlds, the MMOs like EverQuest II, World of Warcraft, Warhammer Online and so forth. That being the case, there's no dearth of psychologically exciting, morally ambiguous, or even recklessly destructive situations within. Losing yourself is never as simple as just a magically "addicting" game. Having read this book it should be clear that the appeal of any secondary world isn't a mystical vortex. The hooks that attract "citizens" to worlds like Second Life, Whyville, There, HiPiHi and so forth can involve a person through the illusion of fantasy. The challenge of balancing such a world is the challenge of balancing the volition of the media experience with the constraints, be they social, financial, relational or otherwise, found in reality. Rather than just the encroachment of an addiction on the primary life, the concern is losing parts of yourself to the fantasies created in a secondary life.

In the more mechanical, designed, and commercial secondary worlds, the line has more to do with the desire to cling to entertainment. When any media experience accustoms the brain to consumption of experience, rather than living, play acquires a nasty face.

For this thought we're going to return to a couple of gamers from Philadelphia: Dave Yeager and Andrew, whose blog posts we discussed in the chapter on motivations. Their passion for gaming has been tended over the past decade by meeting for Dungeons and Dragons, Shadowrun and other tabletop games. After they had all joined, existed in, and then exited Warcraft, Dave invited them to fresh games of in-person Shadowrun. Almost right away, he discovered that what once was "play" was now something new. This group's approach to the experience, built up over the course of a decade, had shifted after being immersed in the experience of Warcraft.

"Even the guys I played with before [World of Warcraft]," says Yeager, "guys I'd gamed with for years.... Things changed dramatically at the table even with them. There was a lot more focus on stats and what kind of treasure the monsters had. I mean it was like the Twilight Zone. I couldn't figure out what happened."

He continued, "Problem is, tabletop gaming is not a whole lot like [World of Warcraft] or an MMO. It was sometimes a bit frustrating, like they'd sit down and be read to [so that they could] be entertained. The best tabletop games don't run that way; there is a give and take."

Dave tried picking up new games so as to reengage his friends, finding that he had to completely escape all traces of the game Warcraft, moving away from all paper-and-dice gaming as equally steeped in high fantasy.

Whether you want to blame repetition, the brain's inherent ability to change itself, or the consumption of experience, commercial secondary worlds are changing the expectations of even the most bull-headed gamer. When players sit down to games in a real space, there's a certain magic involved. There's a challenge to spontaneous creation, a stimulation of creativity that builds steam moment to moment. Only very rarely have game developers brought such magic into online secondary worlds being bandied as games. More often, "players" are made to objectify themselves and others so as to achieve the mechanical goals presented as important. All games, to some extent, mask the presence of other players from us. Should game design seek to make such objectification less pronounced, if such a thing were possible? Treating people well or poorly, whether or not their presence is digital, we are changed in some way. When wanting the next level, the next piece of gear, the next big thing, when desire to consume experience inside a secondary world hijacks one's ability to enjoy the simple pleasures of any world, they've crossed the line from healthy to unhealthy.

No matter the type of world, addiction seems less substantial or tantamount a concern than simply losing oneself. Whether a person is lost in empowered fantasy or designed experience, the overarching challenge to today's games seems to be perspective. Humans are a whole, a sum of the domains in which they live. Losing oneself in the real illusion is never simple. Between what's possible inside and what a person gleans, neither does losing yourself have to be a foregone conclusion. Keeping gaming in perspective means keeping your life in perspective: who you are, who you want to be and whether your life works well. Though this book is one that has to labor over the problems and pathologies possible, one thing should be made clear. Gaming, even when a person wholly falls into the grips of fantasy, or an overly rewarding experience, very often is not harmful.

In many cases, gaming kept in balance brings something tangible and positive to our lives: fun.

The Technology of Balance

Meet Jee Hoon Oh, from Seoul, South Korea. He plays and makes games. Like a significant percentage of the South Korean population, he also worked to become a high-level player in the MMO game Lineage.

"I played [Lineage] most of the time, except eating and sleeping and minimal attendance to maintain my student status," he says, "Moreover, my older brother ran an IGR (internet game room); there's cool off-line community whose interests are same [but they come from] different jobs and backgrounds. It was extremely fun to stay in IGR, playing game with friends."

He recalls reaching the top. "I suddenly realized that I don't have a goal any more. Everything was in vain, slowly recognizing that what I built up in cyber life wasn't so useful in my real life." Later he notes that reaching that realization can be harsh for a player. "...My case is terrible to experience and it's not best way for game addict."

Jee Hoon emphasizes that the offline communities provide a key draw for South Korean gamers. He writes, "When I quit playing game, off-line community makes me to play game again." When it comes to balancing games and life, he's unsure as to whether government policies want to help players to "harmonize," so much as they would like to kill gaming outright. "All of us know that 'Internet Addiction' is serious in Korea, but government seems not interested in game industry. Revenue for game industry is decreasing."

Though the term "harmony" is scholarly in South Korea, insofar as balancing primary and secondary life might go, he says that it can be common to hear the expression, "game is just a game." Seeing the younger generation grow up in such a tech-savvy country and, having learned to "harmonize" himself, he believes that South Koreans of all ages will have an easier time learning to balance games effectively, though that balance was a skill that took time for him to learn.

Looking back, he says, "Now [that] I'm living [a] harmonized life, there's distinctive perspectives between what I could have from online-game life and my real life. If I have free time, especially [on weekends], I enjoy online-MMO 12 hours a day, but I also go out with my girlfriend, meet friends, enjoy playing piano [and] singing. Although pleasure [feedback] from my action is much faster in case of game playing, both of them are great pleasure for me." With a smile, he notes that he and his close friends refer to this status as "pro-addict."

How common is Jee Hoon's story, though? Learning to balance gaming with life, after having been locked into a long cycle of excess gaming? Do gamers "learn" harmony, learn how to set aside the secondary world after experiencing the targeted "feedback," or stimulation, from gaming?

At first glance, it seems to be a uniting feature of gamers from around the world. They describe growing their knowledge of what works and what doesn't. And yet, despite the frequency with which this balance anecdote is reported, it's often reported alongside stories of intense imbalance beforehand. Whether a person describes being lost in immersion, entranced by experiences inside, or snagged by chemical addiction, it seems safe to say that their functioning was impacted.

There's been very little serious research work into whether, let alone how, those playing take steps to balance play. Some early research has reported that ample numbers of gamers self-report having experienced imbalances and that they recognize the problems among other people, though it remains unclear how players monitor themselves, if they do at all.

Can haphazard trial-and-error be expected to act as a legitimate teacher for the skills that help a person maintain perspective? We're talking about balancing extreme forms of stimulation, of one flavor or another, with the basic necessities of reality. A fatalistic litmus test, in the case of balancing games, is whether to sit back down at a certain type of game spells another doom for the person. Whether they'll cross that line, from having some grasp on life and living it, to losing it once again. Trial-and-error learning, that is to say blithe ignorance to what draws you or another individual into a game, seems not to be the smart way to approach gaming.

If a gamer is aware of his own limitations — the hooks that reach up to pull him under — we might presume him better able to enter certain games with better, more effective tools for balance. Say that a particular game's lures have pulled in a particular person, in the past. That game is a kind of minefield. Problematic structural characteristics of a game are like the mines. If a person can become familiar with those lures, we could expect him to play games as a kind of prepared minesweeper. He perceives the mines that he can mark, avoids them, and is less likely to lose a limb. This person will have better luck than a gamer who runs back and forth, flailing his arms, in a field known to be riddled with mines.

The most common anecdote of "minesweeping" among gamers who claim to have learned balance is to flag specific a genre of games as a deadfall. This was the most common strategy of the gamers interviewed for this book. Primarily interviewees had lost themselves, or at least had seen the potential to lose themselves, inside specific game-like secondary worlds online. Using the mine analogy, having lost a piece of themselves in the past was enough a lesson. Despite how focused the anger or sharp the regret, I can say personally that it is difficult not to heed the lure of games, even those whose pitfalls I know intimately. That targeted feedback, the feelings that they bring, are a limb that humans likely can't remove for long. It's all too easy for humans to believe that they've overcome an undeniable habituation from their past. This denial is a classic element of addiction and dependency. Some players go back to the binge situations inside online secondary worlds a matter of days or weeks after having their "moments of clarity." The brain often needs no thought-through excuse to be drawn to rewarding experience.[2]

Some patterns are not so fully stamped into the brain. In those cases, gamers who can grasp the lines that were crossed in the past can make warning signs more immediately apparent in the future. If a player inside a social secondary world, for example Second Life, learns that it's fine to constantly lose themselves in the power they have, some of these patterns can be unlearned. Given the nature of other fantasies, some players should never return; in cases of reprehensible fantasy, the process of psychotherapy and counseling would take great amounts of time and money. Returning to the secondary would be the impulse of somebody who *wants* to lose himself once again.

While the objectification found at extreme levels in secondary worlds encourages a level of play that's outright ridiculous, people with balanced and functioning lives seem capable of entering and leaving easily enough. That being the case, entering for many hours, let alone many days at a time, is not healthy. Binging in games doesn't bode well for your ability to enjoy either the primary or secondary world. Meanwhile, games are still designed in ways that encourage their players to do just that. Binges will always be an engraved invitation for trouble. The level of immersion will always be capable of empowering binging.

Secondary worlds and game design, together and apart, are perhaps two of the most underrated human advancements of the past twenty years. Secondary worlds connect people inside a space. To even provide such a space presents opportunities, for instance in education, that have rarely been considered. Imagine that a 13th century Japanese master swordsmith could use video game-like controls in order to capture the precise movements of his craft, to lay out the specific tools needed. Imagine the cultural, anthropological, and monetary value of such a recorded experience, should it exist. Such designed systems could extend the preservation of knowledge beyond the academic and into the tactile.

There's untapped, even undreamed utility to gaming, but it doesn't stop at photorealistic three-dimensional space. As the design of satiating experience becomes more sophisticated, game design could be applied to problems that have yet to present themselves. And yet, as designers expand their stable of tricks for crafting experience, so grows their social responsibility to ply their craft with ethical direction. Game designer seems an unfitting title. "Experience designer" or "reward planner" might be more fitting, as so much of the confusion in media experience grows out of individuals' diverse notions of correct action in play conflicting with their expectations for correct action in society.

When game companies foist rewarding and morally off-color power fantasies as "play," nobody should be surprised that certain gamers grossly mistreat one another in "real" ways. "It's just a game," it's made too easy to pluck up the experiences you want and consume them, even at the expense of others. Perhaps onlookers should be equally unsurprised when rewarding and morally elegant stories and experiences lead those at the helm to do good things for others, more often than not.

It should be neither surprising nor assumed that individuals who function well enough can snatch up concentrated fun without incident. The stories discussed in this book flit from the shocking to the mundane. Both are important to acknowledge, because both are happening. Sometimes games are taken in with a sense of balance, a sense of harmony within individuals and society both. Our knowledge of balancing technology on the individual and societal level is nascent, making it similar in many ways to game design and world design. The technologies of any media experience will always have a short head start on our knowledge of how to balance them — they've got to be developed and experienced before we can fully understand how they challenge or change our ways of life.

Without the technology of balance, those entering secondary worlds are left with few options beside trial and error. In certain types of games, for certain types of people, that will be like walking through a minefield.

Because media experiences change the way our brain works, the very best way to keep healthy is to maintain balance from the outset. Gaming problems aren't a matter of "prevention and control of a harmful drug," but nor does it help to pretend that a game world never causes problems. Once this process takes a player to the point where gaming gives the brain more than it can handle, once the experience is no longer a part of life but a chemically preferable life, it then becomes a major task to bring balance back to the table. Moreover, if these secondary worlds grow to be as necessary as a computer or car, an inability to balance them can limit the career, bodily health, mental health and the personal life.

When immersion alone, let alone tangible motivation and chemical addiction, provide enough to capture and hold a person's attention for protracted periods, a desire to keep gaming in perspective isn't going to be enough. For the time being the technology of balance comes out of grasping these specifics inasmuch as they apply to an individual's needs. If somebody just watches television, then a greater understanding of visual imagery tells why inane commercials, local news, and reruns of *The Hills* were able to hijack our eyes. Somebody going into interactive "games," well, they need to understand a bit more. Parents with kids who play? They've also got a lot to understand.

When it comes to making this knowledge straightforward for the people involved, that's going to take research and time. More people pick up gaming every day. The whole of the coming generation is inundated. Recognizing pathological play is increasingly a basic life skill. Young people are educated on the risks of safe sex, STDs, health, nutrition and exercise. Failing to also educate on the potential problems in video games will only become more costly.

Games Might Kill You

"A 24-year-old unemployed male visited a computer game room and commenced playing 'myu' game from 9:24 P.M. on October 4 to 10:40 A.M. on October 8, 2002, with minimal sleep and only unhealthy instant noodles for food,"[3] begins the autopsy report. The author of the autopsy remembers examining the body for the cause of death. He notes the young gamer playing through "...nearly four days of board-and-lodging [about 80 hours] while continuously sitting in a chair." According to eyewitness accounts, autopsy findings, and toxicology, the author concluded that the cause of death was fatal pulmonary thromboembolism.

In recent years, researchers have probed the association between long-term sitting and lethal blood clots in the legs.[4] Deep venous thrombosis, or DVT, tends to be reserved for people over forty, with genetic predisposition and other risk factors. Though sitting has been linked to the DVT at various times throughout history, there seem to be few enough people wondering at the possible contribution of marathon gaming sessions.

Researchers from New Zealand were surprised to see the number of doctors unfamiliar with the link in a group of sitters formally diagnosed with DVT, yet with no common risk factors. "In four of the five cases, the role of prolonged seated immobility was not recognized by the attending doctors, despite the possibility being proposed by the patient in three of the cases."

As for the 24-year-old Korean man, "He abruptly collapsed in front of the computer, then recovered consciousness shortly after and made a call. One hour later, however, he was found dead in the toilet."

When a person has obvious mental and/or physical problems with gaming, that shouldn't be cast into the same lot as problems with "controlled substances." It would be equally wrongheaded to pretend that those problems don't exist. Overstating, oversimplifying, and sensationalizing apparent problems inherent to gaming is just as self-deluding as understating, downplaying, or even outright ignoring them. Games can cause problems, but those problems should not be pigeonholed into unfortunate clichés.

Poor nutrition, little sleep, protracted sitting, no exercise, a growing reliance on computers, a society increasingly focused on selling and being sold — games are not the only culprit. The evolution of media experience and its breakneck pace are only one element to our dramatically changing world.

If the mix of sitting without exercise, lack of sleep, and poor nutrition are responsible for problems with the lethality of deep vein thrombosis, if our way of life is bringing on new types of sickness and sudden death, exacerbated or invited by play, then it does little good to either sensationalize *or* trivialize. When gamers have died, in recent years, there has largely either been outcry from worried journalists and parents, or immature outrage on behalf of the persecuted nerds. Attempts at explanation don't get nearly as much press.

When a gamer has a hard time functioning in reality, it's often too easy to focus on just gaming rather than on the whole human. It's also too easy to write it all off as an addiction, in all of its simplistic glory. There are many, many different reasons that we play to excess. When play is motivated by the mechanical rewards of games, the social satisfaction of secondary worlds, or even the chemical feedback of a built addiction, neither media experiences nor physical experiences are one-dimensional. Obsessive compulsive disorders, manic episodes, necrophilia, depression, humans with a range of pathology can find release in specific secondary worlds. Addiction is not the only draw. Neither is the draw of a secondary world dependent on pathology.

Our brains change as we age, they fit themselves around the situations that we put ourselves in. If a gamer spends the better part of each day inside a designed reality, the brain will eventually shift so as to be able to interpret the designs effectively. If a gamer spends time inside a secondary world at the expense of the other domains that they need to survive, then their effectiveness in those domains will diminish. A brain that begins to rely on a "play, play, play" mentality is perhaps more than just locked into the mechanics. Another brain that relies on being able to create and live within any chosen reality could become reliant on more than just a freedom to be anything. What these gamers are building, right now, is complex culturally and physiologically. In many ways this games culture is more than forcibly divorcing itself from the expectations found in reality.

And children, whose brains are quite a lot more mutable and, depending on developmental age, in many essential areas unformed, make the task of grasping these new venues for experience all the more daunting. How they impact online ecosystems is one side; yet these ecosystems also impact the ways that kids traditionally have developed—the whole kid: primary life, secondary life, hobbies and skills. Learning to interact in specific designed realities is a double-edged sword. On the one hand, young people grow an intrinsic aptitude to navigating the space. On the other, their expectations for reality can be shifted in ways that could follow them for the rest of their lives.

The primary world is still a critical slice of the whole person. Our stone-age bodies and our minds weren't developed to live primarily in the secondary. Life as a child is complicated enough, without negotiating the expectations, rewards, and workings of two worlds. Games can be a lot of fun, yes, but certain types of games are complex enough to spin even successful adults in circles. Giving complex games to human *children*, plenty complex on their own, opens doors that we do not yet understand.

Games are, as any other rewarding venue for experience, changing our brains; that means addiction is just one tiny blip on the radar of how games can shake the foundations of our planet. We could never just pitch the current generation out the window—but we must keep an open and focused eye trained upon what in emergent technology assists or hinders them with regard to becoming happy and healthy individuals. We must also learn how people can better and more responsibly consume media— no matter their age.

Instead of thinking either that games are unadulterated evil or a form of art beyond criticism, humanity can and should move on to the next step: learning how to use them responsibly, with prudence, harnessing their utility in ways that makes sense. Games can be good and they can be bad. Gamers play in ways that improve their ability to think and to live, though also in ways that can wholly consume a life.

There is a texture to the secondary world, a texture few have had adequate cause or whim to peer into before now. The contents of today's "games" cannot be touched, but nor are they simply imagined at this juncture. We can ill afford to further ignore and misrepresent their contents, as these contents influence and affect secondary and primary lives. For many the question is not the trite and oversimplified, "how many hours per day is healthy?" but rather, "What have I become?"

Our environments are changing. Our bodies are not. This is the most practical, most down-to-earth reason to counterbalance the pull of media with a strong awareness of that pull. Our societies have yet to truly look at themselves to ask, "Which brings the most joy, survivability, and utility to our race? Knowing that, what is the right balance between real illusion and real life?"

The Power to Destroy

Though society, generally, may not be completely prepared to take in games, addiction isn't the limit to their effect. After more than a decade of playing in these spaces, I like to think of myself as a cultural ambassador. Canadians, Russians, Chinese, Mexicans, French, Indians, Singaporeans, Israelis, New Zealanders, Brits, Scots, Irish, Texans, and that's just one game. Through gaming in general we are connected; I have been connected. Gamers endure high adventure with one another. The interaction is intense. It constitutes a viable cultural exchange, without any primary-world travel.

This isn't just global awareness. It's being connected to people in a way that's going to make me, personally, acutely aware of myself, if I find myself shooting at other selves in a real war. I know whole families of gamers in China and have made close friends who are, as of this writing, enlisted in the Russian Army. Something as small as a game cannot outdate or negate something as large as war, but nor are games without any effect on international relations. Nor are they without powerful effects.

Video games can have a rallying or devastating effect on our world, one that will be determined by those who play, those who design and those around them. In a sense, gamers who objectify one another, or whose fantasies transgress on another's sensibilities, do worse than just hurt another gamer. At times they dictate how the transgressed upon may view certain types of people. In many ways these perceptions are shaped only by individuals, except when the design of the game makes the objectification more likely. On a basic, practical level, those social worlds where players lift each other up more often than they use one another, they could make the primary world a better place.

On a purely practical level, any game that brings players together more often than it drives them apart contributes to peaceful relations. "[Peace] requires a value system that puts the preservation of life forms above all else. It also requires a form of communication that is dialogical in character and transnational and intercivilizational in its epistemological reach."[5] When the value system of a video game is based on the actions of individuals, not just the media creators, there exists the potential for games to bring people together. With so many games that are at least on some level designed to get people working together, gaming gets people talking within a sphere without primary-world borders.

The real stumbling block here isn't that combat is a central concept to games, but rather the designed focus on objectifying other people for individual profit. Secondary worlds espouse a lot of complex factors necessary to promote peace: they're transnational, intercultural, and dialogical. The only limits to who can join come from the developer and the players' government. Theoretically, people from any nationality and/or background could join with any other in order to build cities, engage in fake commerce (that can lead to real international commerce) and to fight. In many ways, fighting with and against those from both similar and divergent backgrounds can strengthen a sense of togetherness — sometimes even with the people a gamer is in direct competition or conflict with. Today's players could herald a generation unlike any other. There could be a surge of empathy. Peace could be bolstered in altogether new ways. Looking at how games could connect people, it's also easy to have practical concerns. Cultures could be wiped out in altogether new ways.

Cultural hegemony: you might define it as when one culture grows large enough to steamroll another. Cultural hegemony should also be a huge concern with games. Consider that gamers around the world are by and large picking up English. That's good, right? English is taught as a business skill; if games help a person to learn, then all the better. Since most operating systems, web browsers, games, and other bits of software are often made in English first, or solely, sometimes their translation into other languages isn't that great. Just in gaming, people from non–English-speaking countries are given an excellent motivation to pick up English: better dings. This is happening right now; in secondary worlds that combine many different countries, especially across Europe, English is the lingua franca.

Rather than let their themes give pause to contemporary cultural relations in Russia, political issues in Sweden or even moral choice in Africa, most of the commercial game-like secondary worlds, like EverQuest II, World of Warcraft, and so forth replicate safe and profitable fantasy and science fiction themes. As players create mannerisms, customs, and unique ways of being, they create a culture based off of secondary worlds, at this moment primarily in either the English or South Korean languages. If their minds become accustomed to culture online, they may become further distracted from culture locally. In-game references to real cultures are vague, confused, and often contrary to how those cultures might depict themselves.

Right now this situation provides players, knowingly or not, willingly or not, the opportunity to *replace* local cultures. If traditions and customs in the primary world aren't transferred from person to person, if even mundane texts and paintings aren't preserved, then certain ways of being will die. These could be simple failures, like losing Grandma Bess's biscuit recipe (which happens to be seven generations old), or parents who never passed on favorite campfire stories (because they never took their child camping). These could also be complex failures, like fewer young people willing to learn the intricate movements of a Southeast Asian dance ritual, or young Finns taking less time to smack themselves with green leaves in the sauna.

Culture is transmitted in myriad ways. Sometimes its final knell is the loss of a particular media experience, though even that media experience relies on some vague idea of what that media experience means —

how somebody from the culture should interpret it. If another media is powerful enough to create a culture and way of living all its own, one that takes precedence in a person's mind, over even local culture — its writings, films, theater and customs — its diversity may well give way to homogeneity.

Turning a critical eye to the people mass-producing culture isn't anything new. Cars, textiles, lampshades, even food, it can all, more or less, be put to a factory line to be created in a timely fashion. The problem is whether people really want culture, our sense of identity, to be manufactured for us by a small group of people with the power to do so. The traditional worry, from as early as the 1900s, was that cultural products, like film, weren't being created by denizens, but rather for the sole purposes of "economic profitability and social control." These early scholars were right to be concerned. Even thoughtful, culturally diverse and artistic cinema and literature influence local cultures throughout the world.

The trouble with "addiction" is not only that it can hold attention to the point that local culture degrades, or even that it engraves the invitation for cultural hegemony to influence a person's whole life; secondary worlds are designed and executed to make money. Even worlds that invite participation and cultural production by their denizens, even worlds that are free to play, and *especially* worlds that weave in gameplay. Small worlds, large worlds, single-player games, console games, flash games, student-made games, hobbyist games: game development is a business. The many early voices in criticizing the "mass production of culture," or culture as a commodity, ring very true today. "Something has been planned for everyone," wrote two theorists, "so that nobody can escape from it."[6] Industrializing culture, mass-producing experience, and thereby creating the same "product" for everyone can kill the singularly effective power that locally grown humans possess in defending their heritage from the behemoth cultural molds — like video games. As American and South Korean games, in particular, spread as a digital wildfire over the face of the industrialized world, it seems appropriate to wrap up by asking what games are creating and at what cost.

Secondary worlds are culturally both positive and negative at the same time. On the one hand, they are commercial entities that require taxation from their vassals and are therefore designed to keep players interested in the attractions that cost money. And yet, the games also allow for these people to break free of the paroxysmal commercialization of today's media. Television, radio, and most interstate freeway systems are a melange of recurring advertisements. Most games give a respite from abrasive ads, though are not an absolute deconstruction of media hegemony in any sense. Breaking away from that doesn't appear possible within the confines of any system, least of all reality.

Other countries clearly see the benefits of doing what they can to preserve culture and power through video games. The Chinese government has invested the U.S. equivalent of hundreds of millions of dollars to present classical Chinese works of literature as online games.[7] While some countries see the need and have the capital to invest in fighting this battle online, many governments do not. Their people allow their children into the international sandbox, playing the games of other peoples.

These stories, online or not, are the legends of our time, epic by design. Just as our knowledge of the recent past comes from books, we may be entering a stage wherein our tales are told in adventures that we ourselves experience. There was a time when cultures died out or were conquered not by violence. Whether from lack of storytellers or lack of books, they lost their history. No matter how brutal the genocide, or how bloody the war, it is not for abundance of death that culture usually dies. It's simply a lack of cultural communication. The poem, the hieroglyph, the newspaper, the television, and the video game are all technologies which can be put to the task of preservation.

Just because it's hard to find cultural criticisms of Homer's poems doesn't mean that the Iliad and Odyssey never took steam from other stories. They were stories, spoken aloud, from person to person. Because of their popularity, it's interesting to wonder whether other stories were not memorized, what we might have if they hadn't been so popular. The ancient story survives so well that even Hollywood cannot resist creating movies based upon their substance. Lasting media appear to survive, in part, through popularity — stories that excite and inspire, whatever their historic truth. Perhaps in 1000 years, will have forgotten about George W. Bush. Perhaps the Gods of *Azeroth*, from the Warcraft universe, will remain.

It will be a great shame indeed if corporate greed and cultural ignorance denigrate the potency either of media experience or cultural beauty. If games continue to grow in popularity, then creating culturally sound and culturally representative video games will not merely affect Earth's denizens in our generation. It is entirely possible that the games being created right now will have a lasting if not permanent effect on our own children. The most popular stories from games may well be the legends that they pass down to our grandchildren, for their gaming enjoyment.

Underestimation. Whether of their utilities, costs, good or evil, underestimation is the largest mistake possible when considering the effects of games. We can call them games, secondary worlds, synthetic worlds, media experience, half-real, real illusion, terrible, or fun. But it is paramount that we examine what those words, and their underlying assumptions, mean.

Addiction is one word with many faces. When applied to games, it lumps together draws which are fundamentally different. Using it betrays our ignorance. Though nobody will stop calling games addictive overnight, it helps to acknowledge the diversity of the things we mean by it. People applying the word addiction should consider it an interim term. Though it may never fall out of fashion, it should. If media-effects education ever does become a reality, then the specific draws of a game should be cited: various types of immersion, different motivations, as well as greater awareness to factors related to dependency, as with gaming binges and life functioning. If any such new, more specific words do ever catch on, they'll do so on their own schedule.

It should be abundantly clear that excess is just one of many unique pathologies and possibilities in today's media experience. These reflect the unique pathologies and possibilities in reality, though they grow new characteristics amid new environments. Secondary worlds make comment on things like the influence of consumerist society and how humans treat one another. They show us what we create when imagination is one of the only limitations to experience. They take us away from our lives, while concurrently connecting us to a way of being with possibly just as much fullness. They are complex.

AFTERWORD
by P. Shavaun Scott

There's tremendous irony in the fact that I spent so many years trying to get my sons to turn off their computer games, then became a digital elf myself after they'd grown up. I really liked being an elf. Sometimes I miss it, particularly on a stressful day when that stack of real-life bills are nagging at me to pay them or I find myself looking at a calendar filled with appointments and meetings for the day, none which look like very much fun.

I regret that I didn't stick my toes into the virtual world sooner, for if I had I would have learned a lot more about the reasons people game and the ways games can be addictive. I believe I might have become closer to my sons in their later adolescent years, and in that process we might have found ways we could do more things together apart from screen-based activities. But since we weren't close enough at that point, they bonded with their avatars and did all their traveling in the virtual world. I worked.

When they were younger kids with their console games, and then teens in the early days of MMOs, I was one of the typically busy single parents who couldn't imagine that I would find anything "interesting" in a virtual world. It wasn't until that fateful Thanksgiving when they were in their 20s and refusing to come to the table to eat, chorusing the familiar "We *can't* right now," that I finally got what that meant. I delayed the turkey and sat down between their adjacent computers and watched. I was entranced.

I wanted to do what they did, and more. They were eager to include me, now that I wanted to be included (I also think they needed a healer

163

at the time). We initially played MMOs together, then I set out on my own. For over two years I embodied various avatars, most commonly as Evanor, an elf in fantasy MMOs. I played a lot. Sometimes I played too much. I don't know that I crossed a line into something that could be described as addiction, but I certainly came to understand how easy it can be. I did meet many other people in the games I played who were having serious problems because of excessive and out-of-control playing. I discussed their concerns at length with them.

As a middle-aged psychotherapist who also happened to be an elf, I know I attempted to maintain a certain observational view while playing. I really wanted to know the people behind their avatars, learn about their real lives, why they played, and what they found so compelling about the gaming process. I met people my own age, some older, and as in every life, most seemed to be going through some kind of real-life struggle that they'd chat about once I got to know them.

Even through avatars, people seem to strive for positive human connections. In many ways intimacy comes more quickly when it's anonymous and partly based on fantasy. It's also a human need to long for adventures, and they can certainly be more compelling in an immersive game. When I say "The most beautiful places I've ever visited on vacation were in virtual worlds," I'm only partly joking. I hope that this book stimulates curiosity, as we've done our best to be observers as well as participants in virtual worlds and to recount our own and others' experiences.

As much as I can say I've loved gaming, I have to admit there's the flip side of that coin. When I've seen gaming contribute to others' emotional and real-life relationship deterioration, I've felt that there is something terribly wrong with the process. When I see people manipulated by game mechanics which work beneath the level of their conscious awareness to keep them hooked into some nonsensical task hour after hour, I'm angry. The more I know about the brain and the developing mind, the more concerned I am about the future.

Game developers create the worlds in which people live, and in that way, they have close to god-like powers. What kind of worlds will such powerful people choose to create, and what are the explicit as well as implicit messages about humanity, the way we co-exist in the world, the kind of persons we become? Each virtual world comes with its own culture, rhythm, and social mores. When one spends time there, these cultures, rhythms, and values become integrated into the internal structure of the mind — without a player realizing it.

But people can choose to play, and choose to stop when they want to ... can't they?

I think most of us really like the concept of choice. It's a nice idea, comforting in fact. It offers the illusion of control. It's often stated that people have choices about what games they play, and parents have choices about monitoring what their kids are doing. If everyone makes good choices, we have nothing to worry about, right?

It's not that simple.

If we look at how the brain actually works, we will see that much neural processing occurs outside conscious awareness (Siegel, 1999). Our emotional limbic system often makes decisions with very little contribution from the logical cortex. When emotional impulses rule our decision-making, our thinking brain struggles to catch up, often making up "good excuses" to justify the decision in the process. This is one reason why people do so many things that appear irrational and self-destructive. It's an important piece to understand when we're trying to understand why people play games and why many play too much.

People are not rational creatures, and some are far less so than others. It's my hope that games can move in the direction of encouraging complex thought and creativity, and move away from "dings," "grinds" and "raids." It's also my hope that as the gaming demographic reflects an increasingly older population, those "S Skills" continue to develop in accordance, and that as these gamers become parents they raise children with those same abilities. Self-awareness, self-monitoring, and self-corrections are markers of a mature mind, which as we've discussed, does not necessarily correlate with chronological age.

Living with healthy awareness means making decisions about what is good for our minds, bodies, and relationships with others, not just at this immediate moment, but for the long term. Whatever gaming we do, let's do it with health in mind.

I hope that one of these days my sons and I find ourselves on an adventure in a beautiful place — in the real world. I know that's asking a lot.

APPENDIX A.
HELPFUL ACTIVITIES DURING
THE PROCESS OF CHANGE

If you're in *precontemplation* you are probably not reading this section of the book. In your mind it doesn't apply to you. So let's move on for those who are in contemplation.

If you are reading this section and feeling curious, you might start by writing out what your life goals are, as specifically as you can. Start with where you'd like to be in a year, then in five years. Would you like to have a different job, finish school, or be in a relationship? Would you like to live in a different place, have a savings account, or have traveled? Write it all down. You're only thinking about it, after all.

In *contemplation*, it's helpful to add up the total hours you have spent gaming — *during your entire life*. Turn that into days, then into weeks, then into months — maybe years. Notice how you feel about that. Make a list of other things you could have done with that time, things that would have helped you achieve some of the goals you've listed above.

Pay attention to your emotions. Write down what you notice. How might you be using gaming to deal with feelings? Do you play to relax, to get away from problems in your life, to feel a sense of being competent, to achieve, or to be "the best"? Emotions and needs motivate all behavior, but this is generally happening out of our awareness. It's helpful to talk to others who are supportive and to read forums online like "WoW Detox." By hearing others' stories you will find things that click with your experience. Communicate with others about what you are learning.

Write out the pros and cons of gaming that you see apply specifically to you. The goal here is to increase awareness and to realize that you have choices.

In *preparation*, you have decided you are going to change. You may know you need to quit, or at least get out of MMOs. It's helpful to make a list of things you used to do that you've given up, and decide which activities would feel good to pick up again. You are starting to realize how you've been using gaming to meet internal needs, and you need to plan for what you are going to do in the future to get these needs met. You are continuing to seek out social support for making the change and talking to others who are supportive. If you are socially isolated, consider talking to a therapist. If you can't do that, spend time in support groups online daily. Reach out to others in places such as www.gamerwidows.com. It's hard for most people to make the jump to action on their own.

In *action*, it's important that you have a plan for your time each day that includes specific positive activities. How much time can you spend getting out of the house with friends? Write it down each day. Plan one thing each day to make yourself feel competent and in control. Plan one thing each day that helps you relax. Plan one thing each day that helps you move toward the life goals you set for yourself in the contemplation stage. Distract yourself when the urge to game is there. Watch a movie, experiment with cooking, get outside in nature. Read a book that captures your imagination. Keep writing down your feelings and thoughts, and talk to supportive friends. Learn to be open. Expand your mind and move your body. Plan one new activity a week, something you've never done before. Stay away from the computer. Make a list of things that might set off the urge to go back and binge in a game.

In *maintenance*, be alert. Follow the path you have created. Observe yourself. Keep doing what needs to be done. Watch for warning signs, and if you notice them, make specific plans for what other behavior you are going to do. Put your experience into words, talk to others, write it down. Name what you feel ("bored, tense, angry, lonely, self-critical" etc.) and do one thing that will help each feeling you are having.

APPENDIX B.
LEARNING THE LINGO

Let's talk about how gamers and professionals actually talk about the real games on the market today. This is a key part of really understanding what a game is — whether we want to separate one game from another or just have intelligent conversations about them. For instance, which games let you play with thousands of other people from across the globe, which ones do you play with a few other people in your living room, and which ones are you playing all on your lonesome? To help us out here, we've created a unique method for separating the different kinds of games that are being played today. Whether you're a hardcore gamer, a seasoned game designer, or completely bewildered, this chapter is going to show you a quick and easy way to understand every game ever made. More importantly, you'll be able to correctly name most major games. We're going to use three basic pieces of a game: the platform, people and point of a game. Don't worry if those three magical Ps don't jump out at you just yet. These Ps use the game industry's established buzzwords for classifying different games, but arrange and explain them in a straightforward way.

Take any game, and ask these three questions:

Question one: On what platform do you play it?

Platform is a relatively well-known gaming term, and it refers to the kind of machine that you're using to play a game. There are a few different types of game machines, or platforms. Before we even break into what happens inside the game, we have to look at where it's played, because the platform is going to exert a substantial influence over how you play and what's possible. For a few quick examples, gamers might play games on a personal computer (*PC*), on a PSP (*PlayStation Portable*), or on a Nintendo Wii (*pronounced "we"*). The two most popular kinds of platforms are PCs and consoles, which we'll explain below. There are also mobile platforms, stuff like a gameboy, PSP, or a game on your cellphone or Palm Pilot. We'll explain those too.

PC, as was mentioned above, just stands for a personal computer, the ones with a monitor and a mouse. They come in a few flavors, and people normally separate them based on the operating system that's been installed, usually Macintosh, Windows or Linux. Some hardcore or professional gamers take a lot of pride in building their computers or laptops from scratch or hand-picking the different modifications or pieces of hardware used. As a result, it isn't uncommon to see computers with extremely detailed metal work, colored lights, and even glass windows, allowing you to peer inside the computer. PCs can be used for most types of games.

Consoles are the game systems that most often attach to your television and are then played with some kind of controller. The three most popular consoles come from Microsoft, Nintendo, and Sony. Microsoft produces the X-Box line, which includes the X-Box and the X-Box 360. Nintendo was responsible for a lot of the popularity enjoyed by consoles, and many people will remember their "Nintendo Entertainment System." Most recently they've been manufacturing the GameCube and the Wii. Sony has been manufacturing the PlayStation line, which includes PlayStation 1, 2, and 3.

As opposed to PC hardware, which is constantly being upgraded, console systems are released one at a time. Consoles are generational, which means that there are usually big upgrades every few years. Different console makers compete strongly against one another. This was especially the case most recently, when Nintendo's Wii, Sony's PS3 and Microsoft's X-Box 360 all released products that were groundbreaking in some respect.

Mobile platforms usually aren't anywhere near as sophisticated as their PC or console counterparts. While this is especially true for games that you might play on a cell phone, handheld game systems like the Nintendo DS have worked hard to change this image. Some of the handheld systems are now even able to play movies from mini DVDs. And yet cell phones have their advantages. The GPS tracking features have made cell games unique, often requiring real people to drive all over real-world cities, looking for clues. And now that mobile phones are growing in sophistication, becoming their own miniature tablet PCs, or the recent advances of the iPhone, we're very likely going to see huge leaps in the gaming technologies offered on mobile platforms.

Question two: How do you interact with real people?

Nowadays it isn't always easy to tell if somebody is playing with other people. Somebody sitting alone at a desk might be going it alone, or he could be playing with or against dozens, even hundreds of other players. Even more interesting, players could be inside a massive online world. There could be thousands of other people inside this world, yet our solitary gamer may nonetheless be playing all on his lonesome. Even so, while most gamers are alone in the sense that they're the only person sitting at the computer, these games are often used for old friends trying to reconnect, new friends separated by an ocean, and friends who might never have met without the game.

If somebody isn't playing with any other living and breathing humans, and he isn't inside a world with has other people, then he is playing a *single-player game*. If you've never really played a game before, then it might be hard to tell whether it's a single-player game. If nothing else, the lack of an internet connection is usually a sure sign that it's single-player. This may not help as an indicator, however, as most PCs in most homes are wired. They're connected to the internet. While consoles and mobile platforms weren't traditionally wired, that's rapidly changing.

Multiplayer games aren't necessarily played over the internet; we're going to talk about those multiplayer *online* games after this. *Multiplayer* games just require that people are playing together. Consoles are usually the most popular platform for multiplayer games, since more people can physically fit in front of a television than a computer screen. There are exceptions, however, and some popular multiplayer games run on a single computer. One example is the trivia game You Don't Know Jack, where players all use a keyboard in order to "buzz in," and occasionally players will be prompted to type in their answers. A real-world arcade game is another platform where you might see multiplayer games. Some examples of popular multiplayer games are Smash Bros., Halo 1 and 2, and Mortal Kombat.

Multiplayer online games are often just single-player or multiplayer games that can be played by a few people over the internet. PC games like StarCraft and console games like Halo are both made to be played online. Oftentimes a single-player game will be attached to multiplayer games. These can teach players the background story, get them familiar with the nuances of the game, or simply provide an alternative to playing with others. Online, the competition from real players does what a computer can't, and challenges players with situations that are always new. The game Star-Craft has been used in professional tournaments for years in Korea, where as many as 50,000 people will gather together to watch players face off in Olympic-style arenas. Successful professional gamers in Korea often make upwards of 200,000 U.S. dollars per year in sponsorship and prize money.

Massively multiplayer online games, commonly shortened to MMO games, are exploding. Blizzard Entertainment shook the video game world by attracting over eleven million subscribers to their MMO game World of Warcraft. The independently operated and free MMO Second Life claims to have attracted at least one million subscribers. These games are quickly growing in the public's eye, and for very good reason. Unlike any of the above kinds of games, MMOs are fully functional worlds. They are the worlds where players sell in-game valuables for real-world cash. People can sail between continents, clash with pirates in the deepness of space, go on extreme fishing expeditions, become corporate moguls, and slay dragons. What's most important is that they do it all while working with or competing against real, living human beings. While a lot of problems being bandied as addiction seems to center on MMO games, these worlds are complicated, just as complicated as you'd expect from a fully functional world. Your actions have consequences that are not quite real, but also not just digital.

Question three: What's the point of the game?

So far we've just talked about the platform where you play your game and who you're playing with. Also important are what you do inside a game and how you do it. A lot of game makers thrive by making new and innovative kinds of experiences, and many games mix and match from the following types. For now, we're going to refer to this "point of the game," or what you do and how you do it, as *gameplay*. While gameplay is a complex topic in and of itself, it's enough to say that it's closely related to the point of a game. Following are the major kinds of gameplay that you're likely to see.

First-person shooter games, or FPS games, let people walk around and shoot things. FPS is one of the oldest and best-established game genres out there. As the name implies, these games follow a first-person perspective. What you see on the screen is meant to represent what you might see as you walk down a hallway, up a flight of stairs, or through a crowded city street. This has been popular for a long time in part because as computer technology improves, these games are able to make the worlds more and more realistic. New FPS games almost always try to improve the visual realism or the physics, though they nearly always have one thing: shooting. Whether it's firing crossbows, lasers, poisonous bile, or a golden gun, these games very often come down to reflexes and hand-eye coordination. In these games you can be a medieval warrior, a Jedi, a biochemist in a hazard suit, aliens, World War II soldiers, or really anything that fires a projectile weapon.

Role-playing games (RPGs) allow gamers to take on roles. Most popular RPGs allow players to select between different races, professions, and their hero archetypes. Players may choose to become Jedi, medieval warriors, or smooth-talking gunslingers. Video-game RPGs came originally from the old paper-and-dice role-play games, like Dungeons and Dragons. Quite a few of the blockbuster video-game RPGs coming out today feature entire worlds, often three-dimensional and filled to the brim with unique creatures and characters. This genre has been growing so rapidly lately that many people consider RPGs to be surpassing bestselling novels in terms of story and character development.

World of Warcraft is a unique type of RPG, because it takes place in an MMO world. What's impressive about Warcraft is that it earns its publisher, Blizzard Entertainment, over a billion dollars annually. If we come back to our "three Ps," MMORPG just combines the way people are handled (MMO) and the point of their experience inside the game (RPG). While most MMOs made up to this point have been role-playing games to some extent, many have also borrowed liberally from the FPS and real-time strategy (RTS) genres. Many new types of MMO worlds are likely forthcoming. In World of Warcraft, characters choose to be any number

173

of fantasy creatures, such as elves, dwarves, trolls, or orcs. They then perform tasks and socialize with others inside the world in order to grow the power of their characters. Only a handful of the RPGs out there are also massively multiplayer, primarily because blockbuster MMO games cost tens of millions of dollars to produce.

Real-time strategy (often called RTS) and *turn-based strategy* games usually test a person's ability to micromanage the economic and managerial aspects of combat (though often other things, like trade and diplomacy). In real time, everything is happening at once. Players use their reflexes and knowledge of the game in order to build the right thing at the right time. Turn-based strategy games are like checkers or chess. One player thinks about her move and takes a turn, then the other player does the same. In these strategy video games, players are almost always presented with a kind of bird's-eye view of a battlefield or playing field. In many games, players will collect resources, using them to construct buildings and military units that allow them to win. For example, maybe they have to build an army, thousands of military units, so that they can storm an enemy castle. On the other hand, maybe they only need to get a single spy unit close enough to the castle so that they can set off a thermonuclear warhead.

There are popular racing games, sports games, simulators, narrative games, and games that are focused on simple or complex puzzles. Racing games are pretty self-explanatory; in them you pilot some kind of vehicle and have any number of reasons for driving fast. Sports games usually feature big names in athletics, old and new. These games let you play as certain teams and certain players. Narrative games revolve around a story of some kind. Games that focus only on a narrative are somewhat rare; however many of the highest-selling games in other genres bring in (or try to bring in) varied levels of storytelling.

Some games stick to just one of the above kinds of gameplay, and some mix the above types. For an example of mixing, a game may combine first-person shooter with racing elements, as is done in the newer Grand Theft Auto games. A game may stick to one point, but then add "mini-games," small games built into the larger game. These can be a simple game of Battleship or a complicated racing game with realistic physics. While these categories cover the games that you're most likely to see, new games are coming out all the time. As the technology in games improves, we're likely to see new and interesting takes on graphics, platforms, and players. As the creativity in the games industry expands, we're likely to see entirely new points to entirely new games. And since the game industry is only going to grow, you can count on an ever-increasing number of new ways to play.

Let's See If You Get It Now

I'll just mention a few games that you might have heard of and break them down in terms that we've talked about. Don't be embarrassed if you're still having a hard time classifying games. It takes most gamers years to learn about their small but important differences. Most players usually learn by playing.

If you ever have trouble trying to break down a game, just remember that every game has three simple pieces to it: the platform where its played, how it deals with people, and the point of what you actually do when you're inside. Let's take a *single-player RPG*, or role-playing game, on the *PC* platform. All you have to do is break down the statement. First, it's single-player. That's easy, one person is playing it. Check. Second, it's a role-playing game. You're taking on a role, generally a fantasy or science fiction role. Check. Finally, it's being played on a PC, or personal computer. Check. If this stuff is new to you, then there's absolutely no problem with feeling a little bit lost here. It takes most gamers months or years to learn about all of the different genres within gaming. As for single-player RPGs for PC, what we just broke down, there are some really popular ones. Some examples might be the Baldur's Gate series, the Fallout series, Elder Scrolls IV: Oblivion, or Neverwinter Nights.

Let's try breaking down some popular FPS games that you might have heard of. Counter Strike and Battlefield 2 are very popular *multiplayer online FPS games* that are usually played on the *PC*. As long as we're remembering the "three Ps," we're going to have an easy time breaking these down. What platform are we using? A personal computer. How do you interact with real people? It's a multiplayer online game, which means that a few players are meeting up online. Somebody playing Counter Strike or

175

Battlefield 2 might be playing with one other person online, or dozens of people. It all depends on the player's preferences and what's available online for them. Finally, what's the point of the game? These are first-person shooters. The point in both Counter Strike and Battlefield 2 is to fight using modern-day weaponry. In Counter Strike, players can choose to play either as terrorists or counter-terrorists, whereas Battlefield 2 takes this a step further. Players can choose to be U.S. Marines, People's Liberation Army, or Middle East Coalition forces.

Another game that most gamers are familiar with is Civilization, a turn-based strategy that's normally single-player and found on the PC. In Civilization, you create an entire, well, civilization from the ground up. You build cities, grow culture, build world wonders, and generally try your best to keep your people happy, healthy, and safe. Other civilizations are also out there, building up their forces, and everyone is trying to win the game in some fashion. It's turn-based strategy, which means that you take one turn, and then the other civilizations take their turns, a lot like chess. While some of the later versions of Civilization allow for multiplayer online gaming, each turn takes a really long time. Usually it's a single-player game. It's also a game that can take a really, really long time to beat.

Where the platform, people, and the point come together, we get games. But it's important to remember that while asking these three questions can help you to get to the heart of any game, the three Ps aren't the same as actually playing. They tell you what a game is — where you're playing, who you're playing with, and what you're doing. In reality, every game is different. The three Ps will tell you what to look for, but they can't tell you when a game is going to have kittens that shoot jets of flame out of their eyes. They also won't tell you about the unique culture that's been developing around games, on and offline.

Appendix C.
Commonly Used Internet
and Gamer Slang

What are gamers really talking about? Many of these common gamer sayings are acronyms, while many are simply expressions. Some of these expressions were created "from scratch" by gamers, though most are words that were simply taken from the English language and modified.

"Ding!"
Literal Meaning: "I just gained a level."
Usage: (1) Ding is most often excitedly used after one has gained in a level. (2) It can be used in order to reference anyone's level gain, or very infrequently as an indication that one has gained in some type of power.

Gank (Expression)
Usage: (1) To kill another player in an unexpected, unfair, or unevenly matched fight. Ganking is only dubiously moral. While many players will condemn certain types of ganking, they may themselves freely engage in other types of ganking. In some games, being ganked can cause a player to lose hours, sometimes days, of effort put into a character. (2) Ganking is related to what is called "corpse camping," the act of "setting up camp" near a player's dead body. The ganker proceeds to kill them repeatedly, oftentimes causing a player to accrue death penalties.
Variations: ganked, gankzors, ganker

Grind (Expression)
Literal Meaning: "Complete repetitive tasks."
Usage: (1) Players will often refer to grinds as long streaks of performing some repetitive task, for instance crafting med kits, mining space ore, or killing boars. (2) Grinds are often contrasted with quests or questing. Whereas in many games players can follow some plot or storyline, however detached, grinding infers advancing one's character by simply killing the same enemies or performing the same tasks over and over again.

IMO (Acronym)
Literal Meaning: "In my opinion."
Usage: (1) IMO is often used alongside another statement and sometimes just literally means that statement is that player's opinion. "IMO going left might be better, because their archers won't be able to get us." (2) IMO is more often used in order to add emphasis to an obvious statement, or in an attempt at humor and/or irony. "Don't kill us all like an idiot IMO."
Variations: IMHO ("In my humble opinion").

IRL (Acronym)
Literal Meaning: "In real life."
Usage: (1) Players use IRL in order to refer to theirs or another player's non-game life. (2) IRL is also commonly used to refer to the state of affairs in the non-digital world.
Variations: RL, out of game

L2P (Acronym)
Literal Meaning: "Learn to play."
Usage: (1) L2P is most commonly an insult, indicating that another player lacks fundamental gaming "skills," and is very similar in its usage to the expression "noob." (2) L2P can be used ironically, in order to compliment a player's mastery over a given game. This usage is very rare as L2P is almost always used derisively. (3) The "play" in "learn to play" can be swapped out for any number of other activities, for instance "Learn to heal." These types of changes are often made in retort, coming from the player who has just been insulted.
Variants: Lrn2play

lewt (Expression)
Usage: (1) Most commonly, "lewt," or "phat lewt" refers to highly desirable armor, weapons, or items within a game.
Variants: phat lewt, gear

LOL (Acronym)
Literal Meaning: "Laugh out loud."
Usage: (1) A situation is humorous or otherwise ironic. (2) Used derisively when laughing at another person or player.
Variants: lawl, lolerskates, lolerbagel

lootwhore (Expression, Expletive)
Usage: (1) Not to be confused with "lewt," or the treasure itself, "loot" most often means the act of taking the treasure. Since some treasure is highly valuable and requires a large team effort which can span many days, a great deal of thought and planning can go into who gets what treasure. A "lootwhore," then, commonly refers to someone who has taken more of the treasure than what others feel they deserve.

Main and Alt (Expressions)
Literal Meanings: Main character and alternate character, respectively.
Usage: (1) A player's main character is commonly refered to as their "main," whereas their "alt" will often be a secondary character. (2) Players with more than one alternate character may refer to these characters as his or her "alts."
Variations: alts, twink (see below), twinks

MOB (Acronym)
Literal Meaning: "Mobile Object."
Usage: (1) MOBs refer to the many friendly and unfriendly computer-controlled monsters within a game. A mob can be a monster, a character, or really any kind of creature within an MMO game which is not being controlled by a real human being.

Nerf (Expression)
Literal Meaning: "Weaken."
Usage: (1) When one remarks that a certain part of the game has been "Nerfed," in effect they are saying that it has been heavily weakened. Weapons, armor, and other items are often nerfed when a number

of other players complain that they are "OP," or "overpowered." Nerfs to characters themselves (for instance to "rogues," "jedi," or "healers") tend to cause the most drama and dissent amongst players. (2) "Nerf" or "nerf!" is a common expression used when one player feels that they are at an extreme and unfair disadvantage against certain other types of players. "Nerf warlocks."

Variations: nerfed, gimp, gimped

Ninja (Expression)

Usage: (1) A ninja is similar to a lootwhore, in that both are seen as taking something which, in the opinion of others, was not theirs to take. Ninja differs in that the theft was generally not expected by others, whereas lootwhore indicates a longstanding reputation of taking many items. (2) Ninja can be used as a verb, indicating the act of taking. "John is planning to ninja your sword, you had better kick him from the group."

Variations: Ninjaing, ninjad

Noob (Expression)

Literal Meaning: "New player."

Usage: (1) Used to refer to a new or inexperienced player. "After being killed by the level 1 rabbit, Bill started to freely admit to being a noob." (2) Used very frequently as an insult, suggesting that a player is no more effective than somebody who has just started playing.

Variations: newb, nub, noobie, "to be noobed"

OMG (Acronym)

Literal Meaning: "Oh my God."

Usage: (1) OMG is similar to WTF, in that it can be used in order to indicate one feels that another player is in the wrong, inexperienced or making a mistake. It contrasts with WTF in that OMG isn't normally directly derogatory. That is, it can be a prelude to constructive criticism.

Variants: Oh em gee, zomg, omgwtf, omgwtfbbq

OP (Acronym)

Literal Meaning: "Overpowered."

Usage: (1) Players most often refer to certain playable characters, weapons, armor or items as overpowered when they give clear, overwhelming, and/or unfair advantages.

orly (Expression)
Literal Meaning: "Oh really?"
Usage: (1) Originally used in association with a photograph of a snowy owl with the text "o rly," this phrase is used in order to portray a sense of disbelief. It is commonly answered with "ya rly."

Pwn (Expression)
Literal Meaning: "Own."
Usage: (1) Used to indicate that one player has beaten another by a very large margin. "Joe's rogue just *pwned* Frank's warlock." (2) A situation is very agreeable, awesome, or preferable. "Joe's computer is so *pwn*." (3) Often, "pwned" or "pwnt" is used as a statement after one player has beaten another player.
Variants: lolwned, pwnage, ownage, own, ownt, wtfpwn

ROFL (Acronym)
Literal Meaning: "Roll on the floor laughing."
Usage: (1) ROFL is similar to LOL, in that it can be used in a number of ironic and derisive situations. ROFL is, however, generally more often used in an earnest appreciation of another player's statements or humor.
Variants: roflcopter

RP (Acronym)
Literal Meaning: "Role playing."
Usage: "Roleplaying" is when a gamer, MMO or not, decides to put themselves in the place of one of the characters that they play. In MMO games, "RPERS," or people with an "RP FETISH," are often looked on as humorous by other players. RPers and non–RPers will often have large in-game weddings, host events with different themes, and generally take on roles. To call someone an RPer can be a fun-loving and friendly crack.

Run (Expression)
Literal Meaning: "Complete."
Usage: (1) To run is to complete a particular task, complete all of the tasks within a dungeon, or otherwise pursue an objective. "Come on, Phil. Everyone wants to run the new Wasteland area!" (2) Running or runs can also indicate that one has been completing tasks or objectives

multiple times in quick succession. Groups will often perform one objective multiple times, often for many hours, sometimes day after day and week after week. "Man, these Banshee Caverns runs are getting arduous!"

Variations: Runs, running, instance runs, dungeon Run

Twink (Expression)
Literal Meaning: Powerful alternate character.
Usage: (1) Whereas "alt" can often just refer to an alternate character, a twink often represents an alternate character that has been invested in heavily. Twinks will often own gear that most other players would never be able to afford and are generally only made by players who already have very committed or rich main characters, or "mains."
Variations: twinked out, twinked, twinkie

w00t (Expression)
Literal Meaning: "Yay."
Usage: (1) Woot is a common expression of happiness, elation, or joy. It is most commonly used after completing a task or challenge.
Variants: woot, wewt

WTF (Acronym, Expletive)
Literal Meaning: "What the fuck?"
Usage: (1) The speaker may be indicating that another player is in the wrong. In this case, the other player may be inexperienced, making a mistake, intentionally causing harm to other players, or they may suspect that player of cheating. (2) The speaker may be indicating a sense of wonder, bewilderment, or surprise.
Variants: WTFBBQ

APPENDIX D.
SEEKING HELP IN
AN UNFAMILIAR WORLD

People seek out a therapist when they are hurt, suffering, or unhappy. Something isn't working right in their lives, and most often someone has suggested they seek some kind of help for it. They often have no clue what's really wrong or what to do about it. There may be an identifiable problem, but sometimes they are experiencing unpleasant feelings or behavior that seems destructive and unexplained.

For people who have never consulted a therapist before, the process may seem dark and mysterious. There's always that image of the goateed old guy with the German accent, cigar, and couch. Fortunately, the process has changed in the 100 years since Dr. Freud got the ball rolling with this thing about trying to understand ourselves.

Most people don't know where to start the process, or what kind of specific help to seek. It's not really all that complicated and we can explain the basics here. There are several types of mental health professionals who help people with personal and relationship problems. Marriage and family therapists practice individual counseling, as do licensed clinical social workers and licensed professional counselors. There are clinical psychologists in private practice, who provide a variety of services, including psychological testing. Psychiatrists are medical doctors who generally specialize in treating mental illness with medication, although some also provide psychotherapy.

While there are various schools or approaches to therapy, and differences in philosophy, there are many basic commonalities. In general ther-

183

apists try to help people understand themselves, solve problems, improve their relationships with others, make use of their potential, and feel better. Therapists try to understand what their client's goals are and use a variety of methods and techniques to help them make the changes that will improve their lives. Therapists believe that it is possible for their clients to improve their lives.

The element that is common among successful therapists of all types is that the therapist works to have an empathic understanding of each client that they see. They are *interested* in the client, *accepting*, and *understanding*. To put it simply, they *care*, and they do their best to listen attentively and experience the inner life of each person they work with. Empathy is not related to intellectual brilliance but has a lot to do with the personality of the therapist.

Sometimes people say, "I tried therapy and it didn't work." This may mean that they had an unrealistic expectation that the therapist would use some magic wand to take away their problems, or it's possible that the person they were seeing was just not a good fit for them. Therapy is not a quick fix, but a process of learning how to work problems out — and the "work" is done by the client. The therapist provides guidance and possible ways to make this happen.

It's important to feel comfortable with a therapist. The quality of the relationship between the therapist and client is perhaps the most important factor in how successful the therapy would be. With that in mind, you should see that in considering therapy, you are making the choice with whom you work. You should speak with at least three persons over the phone before making any decision regarding which you might want to meet with, and ask questions about how they work with people like yourself, if they understand the kinds of problems you are dealing with, and any other questions that occur to you. Remember — you want to feel comfortable! You don't have to grab the first name you see in the phone book.

Ask friends, your primary care doctor, school counselor, or your local community mental health clinic for referrals of reputable people. Lots of therapists have their own websites which might give you a sense for what the person is like. If you don't have health insurance that covers the cost, you may need to find someone who has a sliding fee scale or a non-profit counseling center. Don't be shy — ask around.

So is it important that the therapist be a specialist in gaming addiction? It would be nice, as that would give them a clearer understanding right off the bat what you are struggling with. Unfortunately we still don't have an abundance of therapists who are experienced with MMOs, so it may be hard to find someone with specific expertise in this area. However, many therapists do have training in many different kinds of *behavioral* addictions. That's close enough. This is something you should ask about in an initial phone call, and if that individual doesn't really understand the problem they may be able to refer you to someone they know who does. You should also mention if you are looking for someone who is experienced with any other specific areas of concern or needs, like relationship, academic, or parent/child problems.

Trust your instincts. It's most important that you work with someone you feel comfortable talking to. Even if they don't understand a lot about gaming initially, you can explain it to them. A therapist with empathy and insight will be very invested in helping you and will be motivated to learn more about that specific area you are struggling with.

CHAPTER NOTES

Chapter One

1. Crichton, Michael. *Electronic Life.* New York: Alfred A. Knopf, 1983.

2. Barry, Ann Marie Seward. *Visual Intelligence: Perception, Image, and Manipulation in Visual Communication.* Albany, NY: SUNY Press, 1997.

3. Kenney, K. "Representation Theory," in Smith, K., Moriarty, S., Barbatsis, G. & Kenney, K., Eds., *Handbook of Visual Communication.* Mahwah, NJ: Lawrence Erlbaum Associates, 2005.

4. Barry, 1997.

5. Edelson, E. "Video Racing Games Linked to Risky Road Behavior." *Live Science.* http://www.livescience.com/healthday/602749.html, March 19, 2007.

6. Wise, R.A. "Dopamine, Learning, and Motivation." *Nature Reviews Neuroscience,* vol. 5, 2004, pp. 483–493; Brown, Iain A. "Theoretical Model of Behavioral Addictions — Applied to Offending," in Hodge, J.E., McMurran, M. & Hollin, C.R., *Addicted to Crime?* New York: John Wiley & Sons Ltd., 1997; Doidge, Norman. *The Brain That Changes Itself: Stories of Personal Triumph from the Frontiers of Brain Science.* New York: Viking, 2007.

7. Block, Jerald. "Pathological Computer Game Use," *Psychiatric Times,* Vol. 24, No. 3, 2007; Gee, James Paul. *What Video Games Have to Teach Us About Learning and Literacy,* Revised and Updated Edition. New York: Palgrave Macmillan, 2007.

8. Rawson, R.A., Orbert, J.L., McCann, M.J., Smith, D.P., and Scheffey, E.H. *The Neurobehavioral Treatment Manual.* Beverly Hills, CA: Matrix, 1989.

9. Allison, S.E., von Wahlde, L., Shockley, T. & Gabbard, G.O. "The Development of the Self in the Era of the Internet and Role-Playing Fantasy Games," *American Journal of Psychiatry* 163, 2006, pp. 381–385.

10. Ryan, R., Rigby, C.S. & Przybylski, A. "The Motivational Pull of Video Games: A Self-Determination Theory Approach," *Motivation and Emotion,* Vol. 30, No. 4, 2006.

11. Castronova, Edward. *Exodus to the Virtual World.* New York: Palgrave Macmillan, 2007.

12. Yee, Nicholas. "The Demographics, Motivations and Derived Experiences of Users of Massively Multi-User Online Graphical Environments," *Presence: Teleoperators and Virtual Environments,* Vol. 15, No. 3, 2006, pp. 309–329.

13. Radiological Society of North America. "Violent Video Games Leave Teenagers Emotionally Aroused," *ScienceDaily,* http://www.sciencedaily.com/releases/2006/11/061128140804.htm, November 29, 2006.

14. Sylvester, T. "Compulsion Engineers," Gamasutra.com, http://www.gamasutra.com/view/feature/3495/compulsion_engineers.php, January 16, 2008.

15. Koster, Raph. *A Theory of Fun for Game Design.* Scottsdale, AZ: Paraglyph Press, 2005; Bateson, Gregory. "A Theory of Play and Fantasy," *Psychiatric Research Reports* 2, 1955, pp. 39–51.

16. Gygax, Gary. *Master of the Game.*

187

New York: Putnam Publishing Group, 1989.

17. Bartle, Richard. "Early MUD History," Email Concerning Interactive Multi-User Computer Games, http://www.mud.co.uk/richard/mudhist.htm, November 15, 1990.

18. Malaby, Thomas. "Beyond Play: A New Approach to Games," *Games and Culture*, Vol. 2, No. 2, 2007, pp. 95–113.

19. McGonigal, Jane. "A Real Little Game: The Performance of Belief in Pervasive Play," Proceedings of DiGRA's Level-Up, http://www.avantgame.com/MCGO NIGAL%20A%20Real%20Little%20 Game%20DiGRA%202003.pdf, 2003.

20. Ibid.

21. Chee, Florence. "The Games We Play Online and Offline: Making Wang-tta in Korea," *Popular Communication*, 4(3), 2006, pp. 225–239.

22. Onishi, N. "Thumbs Race as Japan's Best Sellers Go Cellular," *New York Times*, January 20, 2008.

23. Chee, 2006.

24. Yoon, Unggi. "Connecting East and West," Panel Presentation, State of Play V, Singapore, http://origin.eastbaymedia.com /~nyls/asx/SOP_5/200807_04.asx, 2007.

25. Ibid.

26. Blizzard Entertainment Press Release. "World of WarCraft Reaches New Milestone: 10 Million Subscribers," http:// blizzard.com/press/080122.shtml, January 22, 2008; Vivendi Entertainment Press Release. "Vivendi and Activision Complete transaction to create Activision Blizzard," http://www.vivendi.com/corp/en/press_ 2008/2008/710_Vivendi_and_Activision_ complete_transaction_to_create_Activi sion_Blizzard.php, July 10, 2008.

27. Aihoshi, R. "Maple Story Minute View," IGN.com, http://rpgvault.ign.com/ articles/748/748331p1.html, December 1, 2006.

28. McGonigal, 2003.

29. Stross, R. "Freed from the Page, but a Book Nonetheless," *The New York Times*, January 27, 2008.

30. Terdiman, D. "Power Lunching with Wizards and Warriors," CNET News, http://news.cnet.com/Power-lunching-

with-wizards-and-warriors/2100-1043_3-0639669.html, February 15, 2006.

31. Kushner, D. "Winner: Make Your Very Own Virtual World with OLIVE. IEEE Spectrum Online, http://www.spec trum.ieee.org/jan08/5838, January 8, 2008.

32. Sheridan, T. "Musings on Telepresence and Virtual Presence," *Presence: Teleoperators and Virtual Environments,* Vol. 1, Issue 1, 1992, pp. 120–126.

33. Tolkien, J.R.R. *The Tolkien Reader.* New York: Ballantine, 1966.

Chapter Two

1. Gregory, Richard L. *Even Odder Perceptions.* New York: Routledge, 1994.

2. Gerbner, George. Companion to the three-video series *The Electronic Storyteller, The Killing Screens,* and *The Crisis of the Cultural Environment,* Media Education Foundation, 1994.

3. Fawcett, Bill, Ed. *The Battle for Azeroth.* Dallas, TX: Benbella Books, 2006.

4. Barry, 1997.

5. Rose, C. *Charlie Rose Show:* Interview with Thomas Cahill. Public Broadcasting Service, 2007.

6. Durant, Will. *Our Oriental Heritage.* New York: Simon and Schuster, 1935.

7. Barry, Anne Marie Seward. "Perception Theory," in Smith, Moriarty, Barbatsis & Kenney, Eds., *Handbook of Theory, Methods, and Media.* Mahwah, NJ: Lawrence Erlbaum Associates, Publishers, 2005.

8. Dibbell, Julian. *My Tiny Life: Crime and Passion in a Virtual World.* Holt Paperbacks, 1999. http://www.lulu.com/con tent/1070691.

9. Dibbell, Julian. "A Rape in Cyberspace," *The Village Voice,* December 21, 1993, pp. 36–42.

10. Tolkien, 1966.

11. Pinker, Steven. *The Language Instinct: How the Mind Creates Language.* New York: Harper Perennial Modern Classics, 2007.

12. Barry, 2005.

13. Pinker, 2007.

14. Damasio, Antonio. *Descartes' Error.* New York: Penguin Putnam, 2005.

15. Kenney, 2005.

16. Tolkien, 1966.

17. Ibid.

18. Barry, 2005.

19. Plotnik, Joshua, de Waal, Frans & Reiss, Diana. "Self-Recognition in an Asian Elephant," Proceedings of the National Academy of Sciences, Vol. 103, No. 45, 2006.

20. Pinker, Steven. *How the Mind Works.* New York: W.W. Norton, 1999.

21. Kenney, 2005.

22. Barry, 2005.

23. Kenney, 2005.

24. Zimmerman, Eric & Salen, Katie. *Rules of Play: Game Design Fundamentals.* Boston: MIT Press, 2003.

25. Bateson, 1955.

26. Zimmerman & Salen, 2003.

27. Koster, 2005.

28. Ibid.

29. Gee, 2007.

30. James, W. *The Principles of Psychology.* New York: Henry Holt and Company, 1890.

31. Lebedev, M., et al. "Representation of Attended Versus Remembered Locations in Prefrontal Cortex," *PloS Biology*, 2(11), 2004, e365.

32. Arons, B. "A Review of the Cocktail Party Effect," MIT Media Lab, 1992.

33. Ibid.

34. Gonzalez, V. & Mark, G. "Constant, Constant Multi-Tasking Craziness: Managing Multiple Working Spheres," Proceedings of CHI 2004, April 24–29, Vienna, Austria.

35. Bateson, 1955.

36. Malaby, 2007.

Chapter Three

1. Yee, N., Williams, D. and Caplan, S.E. "Who Plays, How Much, and Why? Debunking the Stereotypical Gamer Profile," *Journal of Computer-Mediated Communication* 13, 2008, pp. 993–1018.

2. Koster, 2005; Ryan, Rigby, Przybylski, 2006; Yee, 2006.

3. Delwich, Aaron. "Game Theory (You Can and Must Understand Technology Now)," *San Antonio Current*, October 10, 2006.

4. Koster, 2005.

5. Gee, James Paul. *Good Videogames and Good Learning: Collected Essays on Videogames, Learning, and Literacy.* New York: Peter Lang Publishing, 2007; Gee, *What Video Games Have to Teach Us About Learning and Literacy*, 2007; Healy, Jane M. *Your Child's Growing Mind: Brain Development and Learning from Birth to Adolescence.* New York: Broadway Books, 2004; Elkind, David. *The Power of Play: How Spontaneous, Imaginative Activities Lead to Happier, Healthier Children.* Cambridge, MA: Da Capo Press, 2007.

6. Healy, 2004.

7. Nesson, C. "A Message from Charles Nesson," The Global Poker Strategic Thinking Society's website, GPSTS.org, http://gpsts.org/message-from-nesson, 2007.

8. Ryan, Rigby, Przybylski, 2006.

9. Rigby, C.S. & Ryan, R. "Rethinking Carrots: A New Method for Measuring What Players Find Most Rewarding and Motivating About Your Game," Gamasutra.com, January 16, 2007.

10. Swink, Steve. "Game Feel: The Secret Ingredient," Gamasutra.com, November 23, 2007.

11. Ibid.

12. Koster, 2005.

13. Bartle, Richard, "Hearts, Diamonds, Clubs and Spades: Players Who Suit MUDs," http://www.mud.co.uk/richard/hcds.htm, August 28, 1996.

14. Yee, 2006.

15. Clark, Neils. "Videogame Structural Characteristics and Addiction," master's thesis completed at the University of Hawaii at Manoa and published at Gamasutra.com, http://gamasutra.com/features/20060822/vgsca_gama.pdf, 2006.

16. Charlton, J.P. & Danforth, I.D.W. "Differentiating Computer-Related Addictions and High Engagement," in Morgan, K., Brebbia, C.A., Sanchez, J. & Voiskounsky, A., *Human Perspectives in the Internet Society: Culture, Psychology, and Gender.* Ashurst, UK: WIT Press, 2004.

17. Wood, R.T.A., Griffiths, M.D., Chappell, D. & Davies, M.N.O. "The Structural Characteristics of Video Games: A Psycho-

Structural Analysis," *CyberPsychology & Behavior* 7, n 1, 2004.

18. Clark, 2006.

19. Williams, Dmitri, et al. "Who Plays, How Much, and Why? Answers," Terranova.blogs.com, http://terranova.blogs.com/terra_nova/2008/09/who-plays-how-m.html, 2008

20. Clark, Lee Anna and Watson, David. "Constructing Validity: Basic Issues in Objective Scale Development," *Psychological Assessment,* Vol. 7, No. 3, 1995.

21. Descartes, Rene. *The Philosophical Writings of Descartes*, Vol. 2. Trans. John Cottingham, Robert Stoothoff, and Dugald Murdoch. Cambridge University Press, 1985.

22. Malaby, 2007.

23. Bains, Sunny. "Mixed Feelings," *Wired Magazine*, Issue 15-4, March 2007.

24. McLuhan, Marshall and Fiore, Q. *The Medium is the Massage*. New York: Bantam, 1967.

25. McLuhan, Marshall. *Understanding the Media*. New York: Mentor, 1964.

26. Kalay, Yehuda. "Space, Place and Culture Inside Virtual Worlds," Panel Presentation, State of Play V, Singapore, 2007.

27. Ducheneaut, N. and Moore, R.J. "Social Side of Gaming: A Study of Interaction Patterns in a Massively Multiplayer Online Game," Proceedings of the 2004 ACM Conference on Computer Supported Cooperative Work, November 2004.

28. Jakobsson, M. & Taylor, T.L. "*The Sopranos* Meets EverQuest: Socialization Processes in Massively Multiuser Games," Proceedings of the 2003 Digital Arts and Culture (DAC). Co-published in *FineArt Forum*, 17, n 8, 2003.

29. Ducheneaut, Nicolas and Moore, Robert J. "More Than Just 'XP': Learning Social Skills in Massively Multiplayer Online Games," *Interactive Technology & Smart Education* 2, 2005, pp. 89–100.

30. Malaby, 2007.

31. Young, K. *Caught in the Net*. New York: John Wiley & Sons, 1998.

32. Fawcett, 2006.

33. Clark, Neils. "The Academics Speak: Is There Life After World of WarCraft?" Gamasutra.com, September 12, 2007.

Chapter Four

1. Cover, Rob. "Gaming (Ad)diction: Discourse, Identity, Time and Play in the Production of the Gamer Addiction Myth," *Game Studies,* Vol. 6, No. 1, 2006; Ruby, Aaron, "It's Addictive! Or Is It?" *BusinessWeek*, http://www.businessweek.com/innovate/content/sep2006/id20060915_549072.htm?chan=innovation_game+room_top+stories, September 15, 2006.

2. If you're looking for a basic, accurate, and fun description of actual drugs, then check out the University of Utah's "Mouse Party" game. Produced as a part of their "Learn Genetics" program, it's good fun for researchers and regular folks alike. http://learn.genetics.utah.edu/units/addiction/drugs/mose.cfm.

3. Fernandez, H. *Heroin*. Center City, MN: Hazelden, 1998.

4. McBride, W. & Murphy, J., et al. "Serotonin, Dopamine and GABA Involvement in Alcohol Drinking of Selectively Bred Rats," *Alcohol,* 7(3), 1990, pp. 199–205.

5. Church, M. *Adrenaline Junkies and Serotonin Seekers*. Berkeley, CA: Ulysses Press, 2004; Carnes, P. *Out of the Shadows: Understanding Sexual Addiction*. Center City, MN: Hazelden, 2001; Katherine, A. *Anatomy of a Food Addiction: The Brain Chemistry of Overeating: An Effective Program to Overcome Compulsive Eating*, Third Edition. Carlsbad, CA: Gurze Books, 2996.

6. Brown, R.I.F. "Gambling, Gaming, and Other Addictive Play," in Kerr, J.K. & Apter, M. *Adult Play: A Reversal Theory Approach*. Amsterdam: Swets & Zeitlinger, 1991.

7. Koster, 2005.

8. Griffiths, M.D. & Dancaster, I. "The Effect of Type A Personality of Psychological Arousal While Playing Computer Games," *Addictive Behaviors* 20, 1995, pp. 543–548.

9. Barry, 2005.

10. Gerbner, G., Gross, L., Morgan, M. & Signorielli, N. "Living with Television: The Dynamics of the Cultivation Process," in Bryant, J. & Zillman, D., Eds., *Perspec-*

tives on Media Effects. Hillsdale, NJ: Lawrence Erlbaum, 1986.

11. Charlton & Danforth, 2004.

12. Wise, 2004.

13. For more information on reward schooling, check out Nick Yee's different papers on how game rewards relate to the work of behaviorist B.F. Skinner, or check out the original works of Skinner and Abraham Maslow.

14. Depue, R. & Collins, P. "Neurobiology of the Structure of Personality: Dopamine, Facilitation of Incentive Motivation, and Extraversion," *Behavioral and Brain Sciences*, Vol. 22, 1999, pp. 491–569.

15. Brown, 1997.

16. Wood, Griffiths, Chappell & Davies, 2004.

17. Clark, 2006.

18. Doidge, 2007.

19. Beck, A. "Cognitive Therapy: Past, Present, and Future," in Mahoney, M., Ed., *Cognitive and Constructive Psychotherapies: Theory, Research, and Practice*. New York: Springer Publishers & The American Psychological Association, 1995.

20. Grusser, S.M., Thalemann, R. and Griffiths, M.D. "Excessive Computer Game Playing: Evidence for Addiction and Aggression?" *CyberPsychology & Behavior*, 10(2), 2007, pp. 290–292; Seay, A.J., Jerome, W.J., Lee, K.S. & Kraut, R. "Project Massive: A Study of Online Gaming Communities," Proceedings of CHI, 2004; Leung, L. "Net-Generation Attributes and Seductive Properties of the Internet as Predictors of Online Activities and Internet Addiction," *CyberPsychology & Behavior*, 7, n 3, 2004.

21. For further reading on how technologies act as limbs, check out the Marshall McLuhan citations for Chapter Three.

22. Shotton, M.A. *Computer Addiction? A Study of Computer Dependency*. London: Taylor & Francis, 1989, as described in Charlton, J.P., "A Factor-Analytic Investigation of Computer 'Addiction' and Engagement," *British Journal of Psychology* 93, 2002, pp. 329–344.

23. Healy, 2004.

24. Malaby, 2007.

25. Ducheneaut and Moore, 2004.

26. Jakobsson and Taylor, 2003.

27. Castronova, Edward. *Synthetic Worlds: The Business and Culture of Online Games*. Chicago: University of Chicago Press, 2006.

28. For related resources on more automatic immersion, citations on physical visual perception will be relevant, in particular the Barry and Kenney chapters of *Handbook of Visual Communication*. Cognitive processing of space is another key component; good starting points are J.R.R. Tolkien's *On Faerie Stories* and Thomas Malaby's *Beyond Play*.

29. Lebedev, M., et al. "Representation of Attended Versus Remembered Locations in Prefrontal Cortex," *PloS Biology* 2(11), 2004, e365.

30. From his "On Writing." This is a common thread between King and J.R.R. Tolkien; whether Tolkien influenced King on this point is a matter of speculation.

31. Ahn, D. "Korean Policy on Treatment and Rehabilitation for Adolescents' Internet Addiction," Proceedings of the 2007 International Symposium on the Counseling and Treatment of Youth Internet Addiction, Seoul, South Korea, 2007, p. 243; Dell'Osso, B. & Altamura, A., et al., "Epidemiologic and Clinical Updates on Impulse Control Disorders: A Critical Review," *European Archives of Psychiatry and Clinical Neuroscience*, Vol. 256, 2006, pp. 468–475.

32. Ko, C. "The Case of Online Gaming Addiction Without Other Co-morbid Psychiatric Disorders," Proceedings of the 2007 International Symposium on the Counseling and Treatment of Youth Internet Addiction, Seoul, South Korea, 2007, p. 401.

33. Block, 2007.

34. Scealy, M., Phillips, G.J. & Stevenson, R. "Shyness and Anxiety as Predictors of Patterns of Internet Usage," *CyberPsychology and Behavior* 5, 2002, pp. 507–515; Block, 2007.

35. Weaver, T., et al. "Co-morbidity of Substance Misuse and Mental Illness in Community Mental Health and Substance Misuse Services," *British Journal of Psychiatry* 183, 2003, pp. 304–313.

36. Block, J. "Lessons from Columbine: Virtual and Real Rage," *American Journal of Forensic Psychiatry*, Vol. 28, No. 2, 2007.

37. Nass, C. & Moon, Y., et al. "Can Computer Personalities Be Human Personalities?" *Int. Journal of Human-Computer Studies* 43, 1995, pp. 223–239.

38. Clark, 2007.

39. U.S. Department of Health and Human Services. "Enhancing Motivation for Change in Substance Abuse Treatment," Treatment Improvement Protocol Series Number 35, DHHS Pub. No. (SMA) 05-4081, Substance Abuse and Mental Health Services, Rockville, MD, 1999.

40. DiClemente, C.C. and Prochaska, J.O. "Toward a Comprehensive Transtheoretical Model of Change: Stages of Change and Addictive Behaviors," in Miller, W.R. and Heather, M., Eds., *Treating Addictive Behaviors*, Second Edition. New York: Plenum Press, 1998.

41. Healy, Jane M. *Failure to Connect: How Computers Affect Our Children's Minds—For Better and Worse*. New York: Simon and Schuster, 1998.

42. Gygax, 1989.

43. Clark, 2006.

44. Leung, W. "The Lure of Gaming," *The Straits-Times*, Singapore, November 27, 2007.

45. Rigby and Ryan, 2007.

Chapter Five

1. Siegel, Daniel J. *The Developing Mind: How Relationships and the Brain Interact to Shape Who We Are*. New York: Guilford Press, 1999.

2. Doidge, 2007.

3. Elkind, 2007.

4. Healy, 2004; Healy, Jane M., *Endangered Minds*. New York: Touchstone Books, 1990.

5. Healy, 1998.

6. Siegel, 1999.

7. Healy, 1998.

8. Siegel, 1999; Healy, 2004.

9. National Research Council, Institute of Medicine. *From Neurons to Neighborhoods: The Science of Early Childhood Development*. Washington, DC: National Academy of Sciences, 2000; Hirsh-Pasek, Ktahy, Golinkogg, Rogerta Michnick. *Ages & Stages*. New York: John Wiley & Sons, 2003.

10. Schaefer, Charles E., DiGeronimo, Teresa Foy, 2000.

11. Elkind, David. *All Grown Up and No Place to Go*. New York: Harper Collins, 1998; Ilg, Frances, Bates Ames, Louise, and Baker, Sidney. *Child Behavior*. New York: Harper Collins, 1981; Healy, 2004.

12. Siegel, 1999.

13. Hirsh-Pasek and Golinkogg, 2003.

14. Elkin, 2007.

15. Doidge, 2007.

16. National Research Council, Institute of Medicine, 2000; Doidge, 2007; Healy, 2004.

17. Siegel, 1999.

18. Healy, 1994.

19. National Research Council, Institute of Medicine, 2000.

20. Siegel, 1999.

21. Healy, 1998.

22. Elkind, 1998.

23. Healy, 1998.

24. Ibid.; Siegel, 1999.

25. LeDoux, J. *The Emotional Brain: The Mysterious Underpinnings of Emotional Life*. New York: Simon & Schuster, 1996.

26. Doidge, 2007.

27. Ibid.

28. Ayres, A. Jean. *Sensory Integration and the Child*. Los Angeles, CA: Western Psychological Services, 2005.

29. Healy, 1998; Healy, 2004.

30. Ayres, 2005.

31. Ilg, et al., 1981; Healy, 1998; National Research Council, Institute of Medicine, 2000.

32. Ilg, et al., 1981; Elkind, David. *Miseducation: Preschoolers at Risk*. New York: Alfred A. Knopf, 1987; Schaefer and DiGeronimo, 2000; Hirsh-Pasek, Ktahy, Golinkogg, Rogerta Michnick. *Einstein Never Used Flashcards*. New York: Rodale, 2003.

33. Healy, 2004.

34. Doidge, 2007.

35. Elkind, 2007.

36. Ibid.

37. Healy, 1998.

38. Healy, 2004.

39. Carey, B. "In Clue to Addiction, Brain Injury Halts Smoking," *The New York Times,* January 26, 2007.

40. Naqvi, N., Rudrauf, D., Damasio, H. & Bechara, A. "Damage to the Insula Disrupts Addiction to Cigarette Smoking," *Science,* Vol. 315, No. 5811, 2007, pp. 531–534.

41. Healy, 2004.

42. Gee, 2007; Gee, James Paul. *Why Videogames Are Good for Your Soul.* Urbana, IL: Common Ground Publishing, 2005; Gee, *Good Videogames and Good Learning,* 2007.

43. Gee, 2007.

44. Gee, James Paul, Interview with author, January 2006.

45. Gee, 2007.

46. Messaris, P. and Moriarty, S. "Visual Literacy Theory, in *Handbook of Visual Communication*, Smith, et al., Eds. Mahwah, NJ: Lawrence Erlbaum, 2005.

47. Healy, 1998.

48. Elkind, 2007.

49. Schaefer and DiGeronimo, 2000.

50. Montessori, Maria. *The Absorbent Mind.* New York: Henry Holt and Company, 1995.

51. Ibid.

52. Hirsh-Pasek and Golinkogg, 2003; Schaefer and DiGeronimo, 2000; Elkind, 1987.

53. Elkind, 2007; Healy, 1998.

54. Schaefer and DiGeronimo, 2000; Hirsh-Pasek and Golinkogg, 2003.

55. Schaefer and DiGeronimo, 2000.

56. Elkind, 1998.

57. Ibid.

58. Jayson, S. "Yep, Life'll Burst That Self-Esteem Bubble," *USA Today,* February 15, 2005.

59. Hirsh-Pasek and Golinkogg, 2003; Healy, 2004.

60. Elkind, 1998.

61. Hirsh-Pasek and Golinkogg, 2003; Healy, 2004.

62. Elkind, 1998.

63. Healy, 2004; Hirsh-Pasek and Golinkogg, 2003; Siegel, Daniel. *The Mindful Brain: Reflection and Attunement in the Cultivation of Well-Being.* New York: W.W. Norton, 2007.

64. Elkind, 1998.

65. Ginsburg, K. "The Importance of Play in Promoting Healthy Child Development and Maintaining Strong Parent-Child Bonds," *The American Academy of Pediatrics,* Vol. 119, No. 1, 2007, pp. 182–191.

66. Elkind, 2007.

67. Elkind, 2007; Healy, 2004; Hirsh-Pasek and Golinkogg, 2003.

68. Bartle, Richard. "Building Virtual Worlds," Panel Presentation, State of Play V, Singapore, http://origin.eastbaymedia.com/~nyls/asx/SOP_5/210807_04.asx.

Chapter Six

1. Siegel, 1999.

2. McNamara, P. "Getting Up Close and Very Personal in Virtual Worlds," *The Guardian,* September 4, 2008.

3. Lee, H. "A New Case of Fatal Pulmonary Thromboembolism Associated with Prolonged Sitting at a Computer in Korea," *Yonsei Medical Journal,* Vol. 45, No. 2, 2004.

4. Beasley, R., Heuser, P. and Raymond, N. "SIT (Seated Immobility Thromboembolism Syndrome): A 21st-Century Lifestyle Hazard," *The New Zealand Medical Journal,* Vol. 118, No. 1212, 2005.

5. Tehranian, Majid. *Global Communication and World Politics.* London: Lynne Rienner Publishers, 1999.

6. Mattelart, A. & Mattelart, M. *Theories of Communication.* London: SAGE Publications Ltd., 1995.

7. Carless, Simon. "Chinese Government to Fund 'Healthy' Videogames," Gamasutra.com, September 19, 2004.

BIBLIOGRAPHY

Ahn, D. "Korean Policy on Treatment and Rehabilitation for Adolescents' Internet Addiction," Proceedings of the 2007 International Symposium on the Counseling and Treatment of Youth Internet Addiction. Seoul, Korea: 2007, p. 243.

Allison, S.E., L. von Wahlde, T. Shockley, and G.O. Gabbard. "The Development of the Self in the Era of the Internet and Role-Playing Fantasy Games," *American Journal of Psychiatry*, 163, 2006, pp. 381–385.

Arons, B. "A Review of the Cocktail Party Effect," MIT Media Lab, 1992.

Ayers, A. Jean. *Sensory Integration and the Child*. Los Angeles: Western Psychological Services, 2005.

Bains, Sunny. "Mixed Feelings," *Wired Magazine,* Issue 15-4, March 2007.

Barry, Ann Marie Seward. *Visual Intelligence: Perception, Image, and Manipulation in Visual Communication*. Albany, NY: SUNY Press, 1997.

_____. "Perception Theory," in Smith, Moriarty, Barbatsis, and Kenney, Eds. *Handbook of Visual Communication: Theory, Methods, and Media*. Mahwah, NJ: Lawrence Erlbaum Associates.

Bartle, Richard. "Early MUD History," E-Mail Concerning Interactive Multi-User Computer Games. *http://www.mud.co.uk/richard/mudhist.htm*, November 15, 1990.

_____. "Hearts, Diamonds, Clubs and Spades: Players Who Suit MUDs," *http://www.mud.co.uk/richard/hcds.htm*, August 28, 1996.

_____. "Building Virtual Worlds," Panel Presentation, State of Play V, Singapore. Video proceedings available: *http://origin.eastbaymedia.com/~nyls/asx/SOP_5/210807_04.asx*, 2007.

Bateson, Gregory. "A Theory of Play and Fantasy," *Psychiatric Research Reports*, 2: 39–51, 1955.

Beasley, R., P. Heuser, and N. Raymond. "SIT (Seated Immobility Thromboembolism Syndrome): A 21st-Century Lifestyle Hazard," *The New Zealand Medical Journal*, Vol. 118, No. 1212, 2005.

Beck, A. "Cognitive Therapy: Past, Present, and Future," in M. Mahoney, Ed. *Cognitive and Constructive Psychotherapies: Theory, Research, and Practice*. New York: Springer Publishers and the American Psychological Association, 1995.

Block, Jerald. "Pathological Computer Game Use," *Psychiatric Times,* Vol. 24, No. 3, 2007.

Block, J. "Lessons from Columbine: Virtual and Real Rage," *American Journal of Forensic Psychiatry,* Vol. 28, No. 2, 2007.

Brown, Iain A. "Theoretical Model of Behavioral Addictions — Applied to Offending," in J. E. Hodge, M. McMurran, and C. R. Hollin. *Addicted to Crime?* New York: John Wiley, 1997.

Castronova, Edward. *Exodus to the Virtual World.* New York: Palgrave Macmillan, 2007.

_____. *Synthetic Worlds: The Business and Culture of Online Games.* Chicago: University of Chicago Press, 2006.

Charlton, J.P, and I.D.W. Danforth. "Differentiating Computer-Related Addictions and High Engagement," in K. Morgan, C.A. Brebbia, J. Sanchez, and A. Voiskounsky. *Human Perspectives in the Internet Society: Culture, Psychology and Gender.* Ashurst, UK: WIT Press, 2004.

Chee, Florence. "The Games We Play Online and Offline: Making Wang-tta in Korea," *Popular Communication,* 4(3), 225–239, 2006.

Clark, Lee Anna, and David Watson. "Constructing Validity: Basic Issues in Objective Scale Development,*" Psychological Assessment,* Vol. 7, No 3, 1995.

Clark, N. "The Academics Speak: Is there Life After World of Warcraft?" *http://gamasutra.com,* September 12, 2007.

Clark, Neils. "Videogame Structural Characteristics and Addiction," master's thesis completed at the University of Hawaii at Manoa and published on Gamasutra.com. *http://gamasutra.com/features/20060822/vgsca_gama.pdf,* 2006.

Crichton, Michael. *Electronic Life.* New York: Alfred A. Knopf, 1983.

Damasio, Antonio. *Descartes' Error.* New York: Penguin Putnam, 2005.

Delwiche, Aaron. "Game Theory (You Can and Must Understand Technology Now)," *San Antonio Current,* October 10, 2006.

Depue, R., and P. Collins. "Neurobiology of the Structure of Personality: Dopamine, Facilitation of Incentive Motivation, and Extraversion," *Behavioral and Brain Sciences,* Vol. 22, 1999, pp. 491–569.

Descartes, Rene. *The Philosophical Writings of Descartes: Volume 2.* As translated by John Cottingham, Robert Stoothoff and Dugald Murdoch. Cambridge: Cambridge University Press, 1985.

Dibbell, Julian. *My Tiny Life: Crime and Passion in a Virtual World.* Holt Paperbacks. Available online: *http://www.lulu.com/content/1070691,* 1999.

_____. "A Rape in Cyberspace," *The Village Voice,* December 21, 1993, pp. 36–42.

DiClemente, C.C., and J.O. Prochaska. "Toward a Comprehensive Transtheoretical Model of Change: Stages of Change and Addictive Behaviors," in Miller, W.R., and Heather, M., Eds., *Treating Addictive Behaviors,* Second Edition. New York: Plenum Press, 1998.

Doidge, Norman. *The Brain That Changes Itself: Stories of Personal Triumph from the Frontiers of Brain Science.* New York: Viking, 2007.

Ducheneaut, N., and R.J. Moore. "Social Side of Gaming: A Study of Interaction Patterns in a Massively Multiplayer Online Game," Proceedings of the 2004 ACM Conference on Computer Supported Cooperative Work, November 2004.

Ducheneaut, Nicolas, and Robert J. Moore. "More Than Just 'XP': Learning Social Skills in Massively Multiplayer Online Games," *Interactive Technology & Smart Education*, 2, 2005, pp. 89–100.

Durant, Will. *Our Oriental Heritage*. New York: Simon and Schuster, 1935.

Edelson, E. "*Video* Racing Games Linked to Risky Road Behavior," *Live Science, http://www.livescience.com/healthday/602749.html*, March 19, 2007.

Elkind, David. *All Grown Up and No Place to Go*. New York: Harper-Collins, 1998.

_____. *Miseducation: Preschoolers at Risk*. New York: Alfred A. Knopf, 1987.

_____. *The Power of Play: How Spontaneous, Imaginative Activities Lead to Happier, Healthier Children*. Cambridge, MA: Da Capo Press, 2007.

Fawcett, Bill, Ed. *The Battle for Azeroth*. Dallas, TX: Benbella Books, 2006.

Gee, James Paul. *Good Videogames and Good Learning: Collected Essays on Videogames, Learning, and Literacy*. New York: Peter Lang, 2007.

_____. *What Video Games Have to Teach Us about Learning and Literacy*, Revised and Updated Edition. New York: Palgrave Macmillan, 2007.

Gerbner, G., L. Gross, M. Morgan, and N. Signorielli. "Living with Television: The Dynamics of the Cultivation Process," in J. Bryant, and D. Zillman, Eds., *Perspectives on Media Effects*. Hillsdale, NJ: Lawrence Erlbaum, 1986.

Ginsburg, K. "The Importance of Play in Promoting Healthy Child Development and Maintaining Strong Parent-Child Bonds," *The American Academy of Pediatrics*, Vol. 119, No. 1, 2007, pp. 182–191.

Griffiths, M.D., and I. Dancaster. "The Effect of Type A Personality on Psychological Arousal While Playing Computer Games," *Addictive Behaviors* 20, 1995, pp. 543–548.

Grusser, S.M., R. Thalemann, and M.D. Griffiths. (2007). "Excessive Computer Game Playing: Evidence for Addiction and Aggression?" *CyberPsychology & Behavior*, 10(2), 2007, pp. 290–292.

Gygax, Gary. *Master of the Game*. New York: Putnam, 1989.

Healy, Jane M. *Endangered Minds*. New York: Touchstone Books, 1990.

_____. *Failure to Connect: How Computers Affect Our Children's Minds — For Better and Worse*. New York: Simon and Schuster, 1998.

_____. *Your Child's Growing Mind: Brain Development and Learning from Birth to Adolescence*. New York: Broadway Books, 2004.

Hirsh-Pasek, Kathy, and Roberta Michnick Golinkoff. *Ages & Stages*. New York: John Wiley, 2003.

_____, and _____. *Einstein Never Used Flashcards*. New York: Rodale, 2003.

Ilg, Frances, Bates Ames, Louise, and Baker, Sidney. *Child Behavior*. New York: HarperCollins, 1981.

Jakobsson, M., and T.L. Taylor. "The Sopranos meets EverQuest: Socialization processes in massively multiuser games," Proceedings of the 2003 Digital Arts and Culture (DAC), co-published in *FineArt Forum*, 17, n 8, 2003.

Kalay, Yehuda. "Space, Place and Culture Inside Virtual Worlds," Panel Presentation, State of Play V, Singapore, 2007.

Kenney, K. "Representation Theory," in K. Smith, S. Moriarty, G. Barbatsis, and K. Kenney, Eds., *Handbook of Visual Communication*. Mahwah, NJ: Lawrence Erlbaum Associates, 2005.

Ko, C. "The Case of Online Gaming Addiction Without Other Comorbid Psychiatric Disorders," Proceedings of the 2007 International Symposium on the Counseling and Treatment of Youth Internet Addiction. Seoul, Korea, 2007, p. 401.

Koster, Raph. *A Theory of Fun for Game Design*. Scottsdale, AZ: Paraglyph Press, 2005.

Lebedev, M., et al. "Representation of Attended Versus Remembered Locations in Prefrontal Cortex," *PloS Biology*, 2(11): e365, 2004.

LeDoux, J. *The Emotional Brain: The Mysterious Underpinnings of Emotional Life*. New York: Simon & Schuster, 1996.

Lee, H. "A New Case of Fatal Pulmonary Thromboembolism Associated with Prolonged Sitting at Computer in Korea," *Yonsei Medical Journal*, Vol. 45, No. 2, 2004.

Leung, L. "Net-Generation Attributes and Seductive Properties of the Internet as Predictors of Online Activities and Internet Addiction," *CyberPsychology & Behavior*, 7, n 3, 2004.

Malaby, Thomas. "Beyond Play: A New Approach to Games," *Games and Culture*, Vol. 2, No. 2, 2007, pp. 95–113.

Mattelart, A., and M. Mattelart. *Theories of Communication*. London: SAGE, 1995.

McGonigal, Jane. "A Real Little Game: The Performance of Belief in Pervasive Play," Proceedings of DiGRA's Level-Up, 2003.

McLuhan, Marshall. *Understanding Media*. New York: Mentor, 1964.

_____, and Q. Fiore. *The Medium Is the Massage*. New York: Bantam, 1967.

Messaris, P., and S. Moriarty. "Visual Literacy Theory," in *Handbook of Visual Communication*, Smith, et al., Eds. Mahwah, NJ: Lawrence Erlbaum, 2005.

Montessori, Maria. *The Absorbent Mind*. New York: Henry Holt, 1995.

Naqvi, N., D. Rudrauf, H. Damasio, and A. Bechara. "Damage to the Insula Disrupts Addiction to Cigarette Smoking," *Science*, Vol. 315, No. 5811, 2007, pp. 531–534.

National Research Council Institute of Medicine. *From Neurons to Neighborhoods: The Science of Early Childhood Development*. Washington, DC: National Academy of Sciences, 2000.

Pinker, Steven. *The Language Instinct: How the Mind Creates Language*. New York: Harper Perennial Modern Classics, 2007.

Radiological Society of North America. "Violent Video Games Leave Teenagers Emotionally Aroused," *ScienceDaily*, http://www.sciencedaily.com /releases/ 2006/11/061128140804.htm, November 29, 2006.

Rawson, R.A., J.L. Obert, M.J. McCann, D.P. Smith, and E.H. Scheffey. *The Neurobehavioral Treatment Manual*. Beverly Hills, CA: Matrix, 1989.

Ryan, R., C.S. Rigby, and A. Przybylski. "The Motivational Pull of Video Games: A Self-Determination Theory Approach," *Motivation and Emotion*, Vol. 30, No. 4, 2006.

Seay, A.J., W.J. Jerome, K.S. Lee, and R. Kraut. "Project Massive: A Study of Online Gaming Communities," Proceedings of CHI, 2004.

Siegel, Daniel J. (1999) *The Developing Mind: How Relationships and the Brain Interact to Shape Who We Are*. New York: Guilford Press, 1999.

_____. *The Mindful Brain: Reflection and Attunement in the Cultivation of Well-Being*. New York: W. W. Norton, 2007.

Swink, Steve. "Game Feel: The Secret Ingredient," Gamasutra.com, November 23, 2007.

Tehranian, Majid. *Global Communication and World Politics*. London: Lynne Rienner, 1999.

Tolkien, J.R.R. *The Tolkien Reader*. New York: Ballantine, 1966.

United States. Department of Public Health and Human Services. (1999). "Enhancing Motivation for Change in Substance Abuse Treatment," Treatment Improvement Protocal Series, Number 35, DHHS Pub. No. (SMA) 05-4081, Substance Abuse and Mental Health Services, 1999, Rockville, MD.

Weaver, T., et al. "Co-Morbidity of Substance Misuse and Mental Illness in Community Mental Health and Substance Misuse Services," *British Journal of Psychiatry*, 183, 2003, pp. 304–313.

Wise, R. A. "Dopamine, Learning, and Motivation," *Nature Reviews Neuroscience*, Vol. 5, 2004, pp. 483–493.

Wood, R.T.A., M. D. Griffiths, D. Chappell, and M.N.O. Davies. "The Structural Characteristics of Video Games: A Psycho-Structural Analysis," *Cyber-Psychology & Behavior*, 7, n 1, 2004.

Yee, N., D. Williams, and S. E. Caplan (2008). "Who Plays, How Much, and Why? Debunking the Stereotypical Gamer Profile," *Journal of Computer-Mediated Communication*, 13, 2008, pp. 993–1018.

Yee, Nicholas. "The Demographics, Motivations and Derived Experiences of Users of Massively Multi-User Online Graphical Environments," *Presence: Teloperators and Virtual Environments*, Vol. 15, No. 3, 2006, pp. 309–329.

Yoon, Unggi. "Connecting East and West," Panel Presentation, State of Play V, Singapore, *http://origin.eastbaymedia.com/~nyls/asx/SOP_5/200807_04.asx*, 2007.

Young, K. *Caught in the Net*. New York: John Wiley, 1998.

Zimmerman, Eric, and Katie Salen. *Rules of Play: Game Design Fundamentals*. Boston: MIT Press, 2003.

INDEX